Raging Horrormoans

Raging Horrormoans
Copyright © 2008 by Jessica R. Dunton

All Rights Reserved. No part of this book may be used or reproduced in any manner whatsoever without the written permission of the Publisher. For information, please contact by telephone: 617-297-2543 or by E-mail: Sensoryintegrate@sensoryintegrate.com

ISBN 978-0-6151-9458-5
Library of Congress Control Number: 2008901685
Published by Jessica R. Dunton

First Printing

This book is dedicated to Mom and Dad.

Thanks for Always being here
for me no matter what.

I Love You.

Acknowledgments

I would like to thank my family: Of course Mom and Dad, my brother and sisters: Justin, Jaimie, Jillian, and Julia ("Joey"), and Grammie & Grampie. I love you all so much.

I also want to thank my aunts, uncles, and cousins. I love you. Roxanne, thanks for all your letters. They always make me smile.

I would also like to thank the following people for their ongoing friendship and support: Stephen Sensei, Meghan, John and Bethel, Gert, Maki-san, CJ, and MT.

A Note to the Reader

The views and experiences expressed in this book are solely my own and based on my own personal experiences. I make numerous references to my life with Asperger syndrome. I have never been diagnosed, but after years of searching, and a profound ability to interact with and relate to people with developmental disorders (such as Asperger syndrome and autism), I have drawn my own conclusions.

Perhaps someday I will have a conclusive diagnosis, but I did not want to wait to publish this work in the meantime. I am not a psychologist or a doctor and do not claim to be an authority on adolescence, junior high school, Asperger syndrome, or any other developmental or behavioral disorders.

Introduction

I have always known that I was different. I just never knew what to do about it. I had friends growing up, but also a lot of trouble socially. As I got older, the rift between myself and my peers grew. By eighth grade I had very few friends left.

Wondering what was wrong with me, I embarked on a journey that is beyond the scope of this work to describe, but will be covered in further detail in my upcoming memoir. Check my homepage or blog (links found at the end of this section) for updates. This work, *Raging Horrormoans*, is a collection of stories that I wrote in eighth grade, describing my view and interpretation of the world around me. I hope that these stories, along with the commentary I have added, will help people better relate to and understand children and adolescents in general, and in particular, those who have social/communication disorders. I hope that by reading this, people who experience social/communication difficulties will see that they are not alone, and that they will find my experiences entertaining and refreshing.

It is important to recognize the influence of two incredible teachers I had in middle school, who did more to help me make it through my eighth grade year than any school teachers I have ever had. They were Mr. Creature*, my science teacher, and Ms. Doppler*, my reading teacher. They understood me, probably better than I understood myself at the time, and they encouraged and praised my differences. I am heartbroken that we have lost contact, as they disappeared from the school a few years after I did, and tending toward the reclusive side of life, they are probably happily settled somewhere in the Desert of Maine raising pigs and growing fig trees. When I do make a good relationship, it is for life. Relationships used to be hard for me to make, although as I have learned more skills, I have become better and better with this.

Ms. Doppler had a wonderful way with words and added to my love for them. Her expressions were so creative, her speech so elegant, and even her handwriting was beautiful. I was often captivated by her special style. She understood that I was somehow different than the other kids. She always made me feel that I was somehow superior to the rest of the human race, which came with its own set of difficulties. I appreciated her confidence in me more than anything, and also her understanding. On more than one occasion, she gave me refuge from the world under her desk . . . yes, as an eighth grade student I crawled under the teacher's desk as a way of escaping the overstimulating school environment. When I was not under it, I was sitting behind it, one of the few people she let behind her desk.

Mr. Creature fed my mind in similar ways with words, but also with scientific phenomena. He was a certifiable genius, and he used to build amazing things that would send sparks off into the air and create ozone, the smell of which invigorated me. He used to have a sign on his black board that said, "The floggings will continue until morale improves." I never understood that, but I think I get it now. I used to read it over and over again. He often gave me old outdated science books that had been thrown away from libraries. I would read them and ask him questions. He would discuss things with me for hours. He used to write my grade in code on my papers. One time, he wrote *yb*, which I found to be the scientific name for ytterbium, #70 on the periodic table, which I had at one point nearly memorized.

I played basketball all through middle school. I struggled to work with my teammates, and I always felt criticized by them. I was different somehow, in great big ways, but I could not say how at the time. I just knew that I was physically stronger, and had a never ending resolve to win and do my best that also set me apart. We did not understand each other. And that made life difficult. I loved basketball, but I dreaded my teammates.

And sometimes games would get canceled. I could not deal with schedule changes very well at all. When a game would get canceled, I would cry and it was terribly upsetting. I am just getting to the point now, where I am able to accept that schedule changes happen regardless, no matter how much we try to prevent them, although this always causes some degree of upset. The sooner I am able to return to a normal schedule, the better life feels.

This book is a culmination of my middle school experiences. It shows the framework of my teenage life, and paints a very good picture of the everyday world I was living in.

*These were not their real names.

Cast

I am the *Innocent Bystandard** in this story. I always felt like an innocent bystander, which I used to pronounce *Bystandard*. It is pretty funny now, and kind of ironic, because it makes sense in a way, that I was the one standing by, and I was the standard by which I expected everyone else to measure themselves. I was never really able to connect with the crowd, especially by eighth grade. I had lost most of my friends to their hormones and (what I considered to be) strange social groups. Everyone was changing, and there I was, standing by and watching. I did not understand why they were changing or what precipitated the changes. I just knew that they were . . . and quickly . . .

The term *horrormoaner* refers to the kids at school whose hormones were out of control, raging, if you will. They functioned solely from their emotions. I believe that was a term coined by Ms. Doppler, although I do not remember exactly. They were like a wild fire that could not be stopped, and the only thing that I could do was stand by and watch, often mortified by their behavior. Ironically, my pronunciation of the word *hormone*, matched more closely to the spelling of *horror moan*, thus, *horrormoan*. I never really knew any differently until I started examining this work, and the word was flagged by the spell checker. I find it interesting because that is exactly what I saw hormones do to people, turn them into *horrormoaners*.

The *SeeMeHearMes* were the loud kids. They were the ones who did whatever it took to get attention at any cost. Some of them were also *horrormoaners*. Given the nature of my sensory issues, I did not do well in the same room as them, let alone communicating with them. *Testosterhome* is an analogy for the environment that was created by an excess of teenage hormones, and it is the land where the *horromoaners* spent most of their time.

*In a few stories, the Innocent Bystandard represents others who were similar to me.

Structure of this work

This book is split into three *parts*, the first two focusing on different aspects of my life at school, and the third focusing on the community. Each part is separated into *sections*, which are each their own individual *scenarios* depicting events, some of which were more or less real, and others which were completely imagined. The parts that were imagined were based on what I thought could happen given the "strange" behavior I was observing from my peers. The structure of each of the *sections* is consistent throughout. The stories are told using three short paragraphs, each labeled *setting,* which gives the background of the situation, *climax,* which tells the high point of the story, and *conclusion,* which shows how things ended up.

These stories are like little snippets, synopses of what was going on inside my head at the time. Each of these stories could very easily become its own full length chapter, or novel even. I wrote these in such a way so as to use as little language as possible to convey what was going on inside my head. To help with this, I have added pictures and given some explanation about where the stories came from after each one. I have tried to give as much detail as possible to explain what I might have been thinking and feeling at the time. I have also tried to capture the essence without explaining every word and line. In addition, I have included spaces throughout the book for the reader to make notes.

Please remember that these stories are written in my own words in the way that I saw things through my own eyes when I was fourteen years old and in the eighth grade. I have chosen to leave the words, grammar, etc., pretty much the way they were when I originally wrote them. I have however, made notes to reference certain words or phrases that may be unclear.

The way I expressed myself through these stories was how I experienced the world around me, and I want to give people who work with children and adolescents with social deficits, a look at the world through their eyes, and for those who work with people with communication difficulties, I want to show that what they may see from their behavior or hear from their words, is likely not the whole story.

I ask the reader to keep in mind that I spoke in a lot of metaphor when I wrote these stories, often using the events going on around me to explain the concurrent strange behaviors. Use your imagination on parts that are unclear. I hope that you will paint for yourself your own picture. There are an infinite number of possibilities happening all at once in some of these stories. That is part of what makes them special.

There are some places which may be confusing to the reader. After reading through the book, if there is anything that is unclear or warrants further discussion, please feel free to ask me. My contact information can be found below. Also, don't forget to check my homepage and blog for updates on this and other projects.

Jessica R. Dunton

Telephone:	(617) 297-2543
E-mail:	Sensoryintegrate@sensoryintegrate.com
Web Page:	www.sensoryintegrate.com
Blog:	www.aspergerandme.blogspot.com

Raging Horrormoans

Raging Horrormoans

Raging Horrormoans is a collection of my experiences during a typical day in middle school. Most of these stories are based on things (often times more than one instance per story) that actually happened. Each of the Section titles was carefully chosen to reflect what I saw during the day. By carefully chosen, I mean, I thought about them until I found titles I liked, and then I wrote about them. I also incorporated a lot of clever word play.

Section I	Juice at the Water Fountain
Section II	Hearing Hall the News
Section III	As the Stomach Churns the Lunchroom
Section IV	Scientifically Speaking
Section V	Abhoring Time of Day
Section VI	Classroom Cavities
Section VII	Looking at Locker Legacies
Section VIII	English Endeavors
Section IX	Reading Between the Lines
Section X	The After Math
Section XI	Socially Studying
Section XII	The Art of Expression

Section XIII	Bathroom Break
Section XIV	Power Placement Pleas
Sectoin XV	Physical Education
Section XVI	Busride Badgering
Section XVII	Cafeteria Crisis
Section XVIII	Toe Jammed Teacher
Section XIX	What Work?
Section XX	Relatively Speaking
Section XXI	Rapid Redundancy
Section XXII	Personal Problems
Section XXIII	Trivial Complaints
Section XXIV	Instant Gratification
Section XXV	Going Home Economically
Section XXVI	Keying in on Bored Cells
Section XXVII	Rough Drifts are Due Tomorrow
Section XXVIII	Intellectual Inequalities
Section XXIX	Petrifying Predicaments
Section XXX	Arbitrary Annihilation
Section XXXI	A Notable Falling

Section I
Juice at the Water Fountain

Setting: Innocent Bystandards and horrormoaners at water fountain. Water is flowing, but no one is drinking. The onlookers observe, scrutinizing every breathing moment. The horrormoaners stand, jump, scream, shout, and discuss uncivilly occurring events that may cause psychological damage and create future problems if it was brought out and tossed around.

Climax: Horrormoaners spit water at the onlooker because a comment was made about the intellectual development of conversation at the water fountain. Also, he found out that she didn't say anything to him about her, and it was really him who told her to tell her that she couldn't do this because of that and he had had it.

Conclusion: All horrormoaners disperse and the majority are late.

Comments

The kids always gathered around the water fountains. I can remember being in the hallway and watching the kids supposedly getting a drink of water, but they were not really getting a drink. They would push the button down, and water would be coming out while they would be discussing whatever happened to be the hot topic of the day, from their own personal problems or somebody's new boyfriend, to what kind of trouble someone was in.

This was a huge place to catch up on the gossip—or perhaps create some. The kids were loud and obnoxious, and I just did not understand them. My role was not a part of the group, but rather, I was a separate observer. I was constantly commenting on what I believed to be their inferiority to me and other more capable human beings. Because I was not experiencing it, I did not realize that what was happening with them was completely normal. I hated seeing them behave that way, because to me it was just a waste of time. The water fountain was for the purpose of quenching thirst, not catching up on the news of the day.

I rarely made comments to any of them, but I always had one ready to go, and others lined up in my arsenal, should the occasion arise. I wanted to say to them, "the level of this conversation is just above the development of worm brains." I imagine they might have spit water at me, since they were spitting it everywhere else. Also, they were always late for class (because of these water fountain gatherings), and that always drove me nuts.

Section II
Hearing Hall the News

Setting: Horrormoaners and Innocent Bystandards are out in the hallway. Many are buzzing by, but a drain would suffice to unclog the masses.

Climax: Innocent Bystandard gets run down by a horrormoaner. Also, she's breaking up with him because she said he said that she told him that he told her saying that it just wasn't meant to be and the note was found in the hall where it hall* was made clear.

Conclusion: A break up happened and moping was the tone for the next few minutes (until the next problem came along).

Comments

*hall = all

I hated walking through the hallways in between classes because they were packed with people running all over the place who were loud, obnoxious, and just plain rude. They would get in each others' faces and sometimes in my face, and I did not understand what they were doing, and that made me really uncomfortable. So I mostly tried to avoid them.

They were always getting together and breaking up and getting together again and breaking up again. To me, it was absolutely pointless, such a waste of time. I did not understand why they were so interested in each other.

And I definitely did not understand the conversations they were having about it.

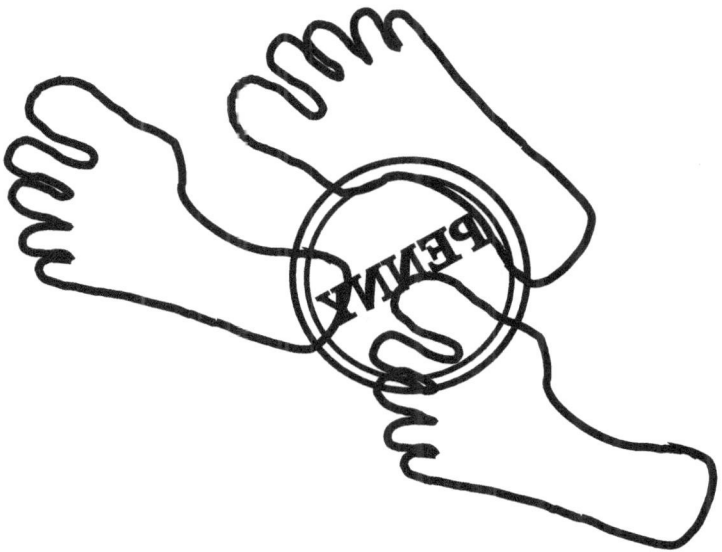

Section III
As the Stomach Churns the Lunchroom

Setting: In the upstairs lunchroom, horrormoaners mingle and speak of his new girlfriend. Innocent Bystandards are on the opposite side of the room searching intently trying to create sense of the whole saga. None is discovered except for the penny everyone is stepping over.

Climax: He told her that she could not participate in that or this would happen and the unfortunate incident* of that activity would cause friction in the specified tasks arranged. She didn't like him telling her this, so she told him adios.

Conclusion: She decided to get back together with him because they would gain more fringe benefits and money.

Comments

*incident = consequence

I used to eat lunch upstairs with Mr. Creature and Ms. Doppler, and a couple of other kids. It was quiet up there, and I found the conversation intellectually stimulating. Sometimes the other kids would come upstairs though, and they would hang around in the hallway and the bathroom and continue their senseless noisy chatter. And in reading this, although it is very general and does not make a lot of sense, that is what the other kids' conversations sounded like to me. Therefore, I really could not understand why they were having them.

There were definitely times when I wished I was not so confused. But most of the time I did not even know I was confused, just uncomfortable. And I did not know why. Incidentally, I would often do things like notice a piece of change on the floor and spend time thinking about how it got there, whether or not I should actually pick it up (or if I should save the good luck for someone else), and if I were to pick it up, whether or not I should keep it or put it back so someone else might have a chance at good luck too. This seemed much more interesting than whatever my peers were talking about.

Section IV
Scientifically Speaking

Setting: Science class has grown invisible to the horrormoaners*. They unobstrusively interrupt irreguardless of the activities happening around them. The Innocent Bystandards jump at the opportunity to in any way embarrass or surprise the horrormoaners.

Climax: Horrormoaners not paying attention; except to the trivial pursuit of happiness (that they never find). Innocent Bystandard realizes this and tortures the horrormoaner with brain power and wit while they just sit there staring, not knowing fully the humiliation that hit them.

Conclusion: All horrormoaners face their wrath of escaping the school world and finally catch wind of their deservance**.

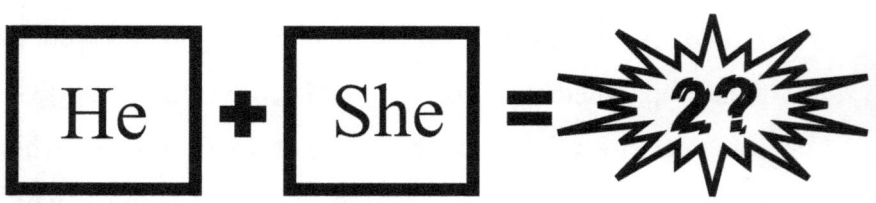

Comments

*"Science class has grown invisible to the horrormoaners," means that they were oblivious to the fact that it was going on around them.

**deservance = to get what they deserved

I loved science class. Mr. Creature taught it. Most of the other kids were just so stupid in my opinion. I wanted to move on to more advanced material, such as chemical reactions (not the chemistry of relationships that the other kids preferred to talk about . . .) and physics, but instead we had to talk about handing in homework. He used to say "irreguardless" (which is not supposed to be a word) all the time, and he and Ms. Doppler both talked often about how human beings have the right to life, liberty, and the pursuit of happiness.

I was angry that those kids were stepping all over each others' toes, all over the teachers' toes, and all over my toes. How could I possibly be happy if they were infringing on my rights? And why could they not understand that what they were doing was so upsetting to me? I wanted to get them back somehow, to embarrass them or just have them realize that I was superior to them. I wanted them to get what they deserved, which was not happiness, because they did not seem to be letting anybody else have it either.

I somehow felt vindicated though in Mr. Creature's class, because although he had a soft heart, he had a bit of a cynical side to him, and he did not hesitate to rub the reality of life in kids' faces. It was one place where I could be superior and where I felt like I was okay.

Science = Fun

NOTES

Section V
Abhoring Time of Day

Setting: Innocent Bystandards, who know what they're talking about, manipulate others to get into the abhor time of their choice. The horrormoaners try to do the same.

Climax: Horrormoaners can't seem to figure out where they are going. They are clueless! The problem is, they can't figure out who goes where because she went into her abhor time yesterday. She just couldn't understand the sappy way of going about them. Innocent Bystandard stepped in and bluntly told her she was just a seedling. That made her pitch a fit. She stomped and barked. (Innocent Bystandard has left.) She tried to get her friend to leave to go to abhor time with her.

Conclusion: Horrormoaners become late for class and Innocent Bystandard smiles with smug satisfaction.

To Tree . . . or not to Tree. . .

That is the Question.

Comments

We had an independent reading program at school. Each class had a different name, which was based on a three-year rotation, so the groups of names never repeated during a student's time in middle school. When I was in sixth grade, we were ships, and I was in the Galleon group. In seventh grade, we were space shuttles. I was in Endeavor. In eighth grade, we were trees. I was in Maple, but I always wanted to be in Oak, because that is where a lot of the smart kids were, and the ones who I could still consider my friends. In sixth grade, our independent reading time was called dock time, in seventh grade, shuttle time, and in eighth grade, arbor time. In eighth grade, because certain math and honors classes complicated schedules, this allowed for another group of kids, referred to as "boppers."

Boppers often went to classes with other arbor groups because of their strange schedules. There were often conflicts. So in order to get the classes they needed, they would go to classes at different times. I was a bopper, and I often chose my daily schedule from the a' la class menu. Sometimes I skipped classes and went to others twice, especially if a certain class was particularly boring (or particularly interesting). I liked being a bopper because I could join whichever group I felt most comfortable with. And yes, there were teachers who did not like me doing this. But most of them had better things to do than worry about me. And I found that those who did make threats could be placated relatively easily.

Most boppers, because they were in honors classes, were considered to be the smart kids. Needless to say at this point, most of the horrormoaners were not boppers, although there were a couple of exceptions. The horrormoaners wanted to bop around to different classes too though, but for completely different reasons. They wanted to follow some peer group around, and create a ruckus, or worse, kiss and touch each other.

I really enjoyed playing with words and with language in eighth grade, as can be observed in the above story, the theme being trees. It was one thing that kept my mind occupied, so I did not have to think about what was going on around me, which was extremely overwhelming a majority of the time.

The horrormoaning kids always used to be late for class because they were chasing each other around. Then the teachers would get mad and give them a detention or something. It just did not make any sense to me. It was the same nonsense day after day.

Section VI
Classroom Cavities

Setting: In the classroom many gather to discuss the ongoing story of how he broke up with her. The Innocent Bystandards, this time (as usual) discreetly eavesdrop so to know uncaringly what's going on. The horrormoaners complain and just don't understand.

Climax: She didn't understand why he said that he wouldn't do this for them when they broke up because he said that she said that we saw how they said that she said we could still write her a note, stating the typical note written by a horrormoaner*.

Conclusion: Innocent Bystandards get to drill at the horrormoaners, teaching them about respect and how it must be earned.

Comments

*They were always writing notes and talking about going out and breaking up. Who cares?

I could listen to four or five conversations going on at once, and although I did not care about what they were talking about, I was intensely curious. Even though I was not able to connect to them on an emotional level, the stories they told were somehow addicting, and I could hear four or five at a time, which I found rather interesting, because I often got many different view points on the same story all at once.

I always wanted to teach them how life should be, how they should behave, and how they should not talk during class or go screaming through the hallways. I wanted them to understand that.

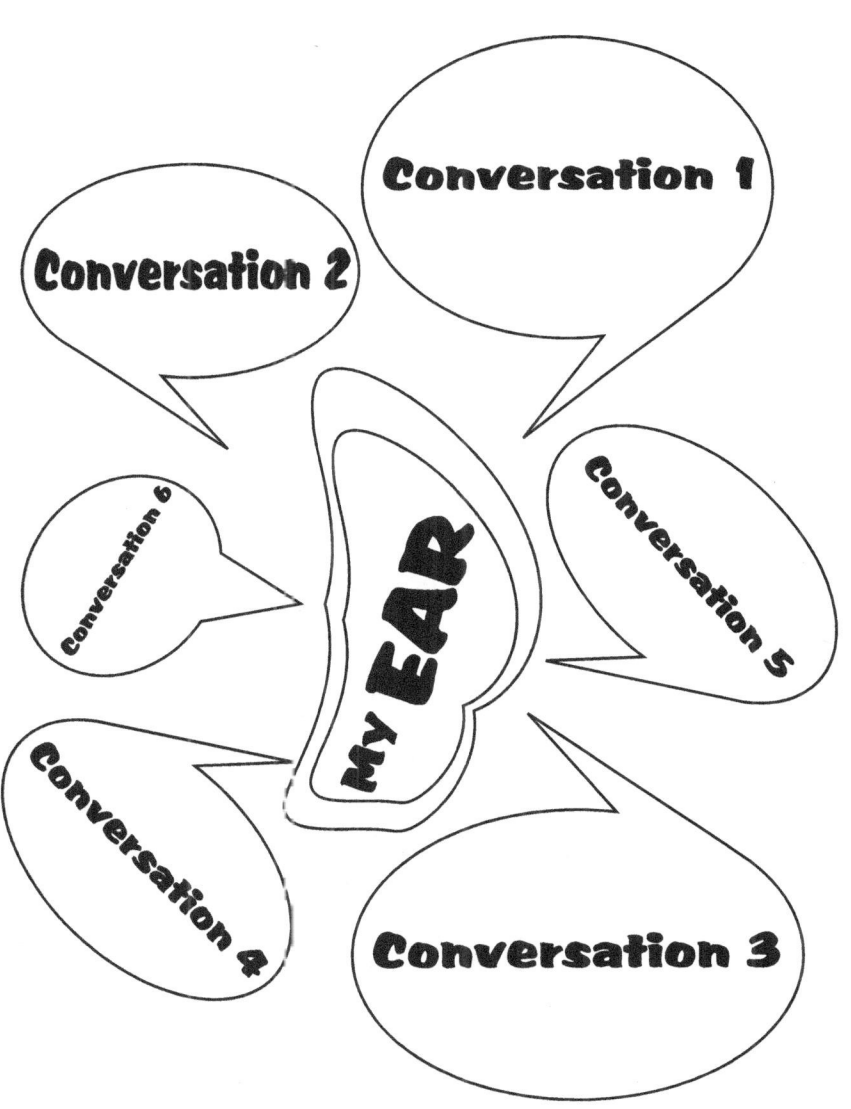

Section VII
Looking at Locker Legacies

Setting: Horrormoaners are huddled tightly around Innocent Bystandard's locker. Innocent Bystandard needs to (as after every class) get books out.

Climax: Horrormoaners give Innocent Bystandard a hard time and Innocent Bystandard vocally humiliates each and every one of the horrormoaners.

Conclusion: Each of the horrormoaners disperses in the same direction to find some other lockers to huddle around.

Comments

They always used to hang around the lockers. They used to crowd my locker, and it irritated me because I had trouble getting my things out. I rarely said anything to them, because I did not know what to say or how to go about saying it. I did not even know what they were doing there. But I wanted to say things a lot of times. I imagined humiliating them all one by one, but I do not remember ever actually doing so. However, I would not hesitate to slip in a sharp comment or two if given the chance. I think on a number of occasions they got the idea though that they were not welcome in my space (especially behaving as strangely as they were . . .), and they would wander off and huddle around other lockers.

Section VIII
English Endeavors

Setting: Two groups of horrormoaners clump into different corners of the room plotting against each other. Innocent Bystandards are doing what they do best—standing by and listening innocently.

Climax: Horrormoaning groups approach each other. One group wanted to know why he said that she said the she'd heard that he'd heard that she said something she didn't. The other group defended by saying that he didn't say that she said that she'd heard that he'd heard that she said something.

Conclusion: All horrormoaners get kicked out of class and are forced to work out their problems in the guidance office.

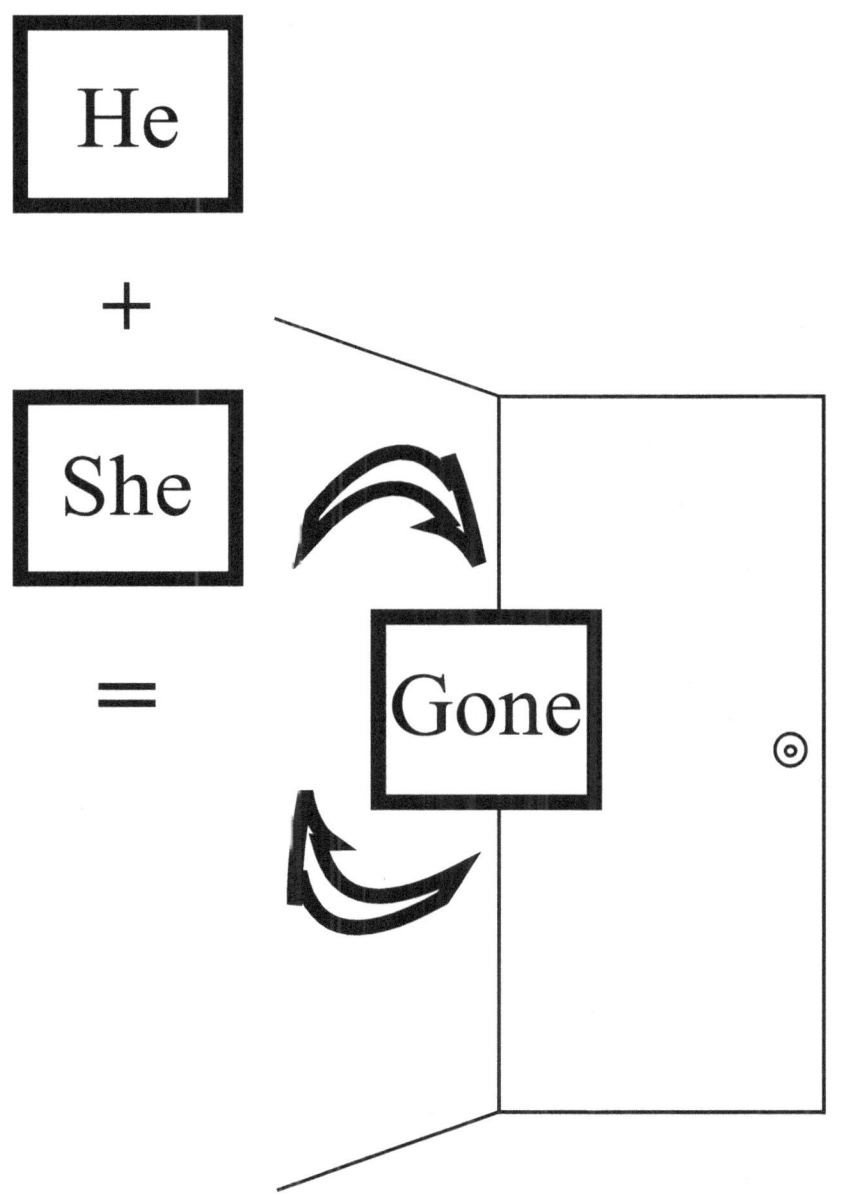

Comments

This was a common scene too. Not only were they talking to each other about who likes who, and who said what, but they were also fighting with each other—whole groups of them. And sometimes it was so distracting that the teacher could not get the class started. The teacher would send them all down to the guidance office and life would continue.

C'mon, what could be more important than learning how to diagram and connect chemical formulas?!?

Section IX
Reading Between the Lines

Setting: Horrormoaners are once again in the classroom. Right before lunch, the moaner's stories are brewing and the saga continues. The Innocent Bystandard sees the restlessness of the crew. The Innocent Bystandard nonchalantly asks the wailing horrormoaner why they engage in such idiotic practices.

Climax: Restless horrormoaners lose all sense of reality (that they'd never known) and become entwined in Innocent Bystandard's trap. Restless horrormoaner doesn't know which way is which (that's nothing too new—but worse than usual!)

Conclusion: Restless horrormoaners miss lunch because they can't understand they must calm down. Finally, they all dehydrate and are released.

Comments

This is probably one of the best passages I wrote demonstrating my inability to interact with my peers and the fact that I was unable to connect with them on an emotional level.

Here I label their perfectly normal developmental tendencies as "idiotic practices." I say that they are the ones who had lost all sense of reality, when in fact it was I who was living in a very different place than any of them. I also said that, "They can't understand that they must calm down." This is a very clear place where I did not "understand," why they could not "understand," and just stop all the nonsense they were doing, and just calm down (emotionally), and work. I was not able to see that they were responding on an emotional level, and it was not a matter of understanding at all, but rather of learning how to properly deal with their own emotions and feelings. It was an emotional thing, which could not be understood or comprehended.

I just wanted to step on them all like bugs so they would be quiet, and not so annoying and disturbing.

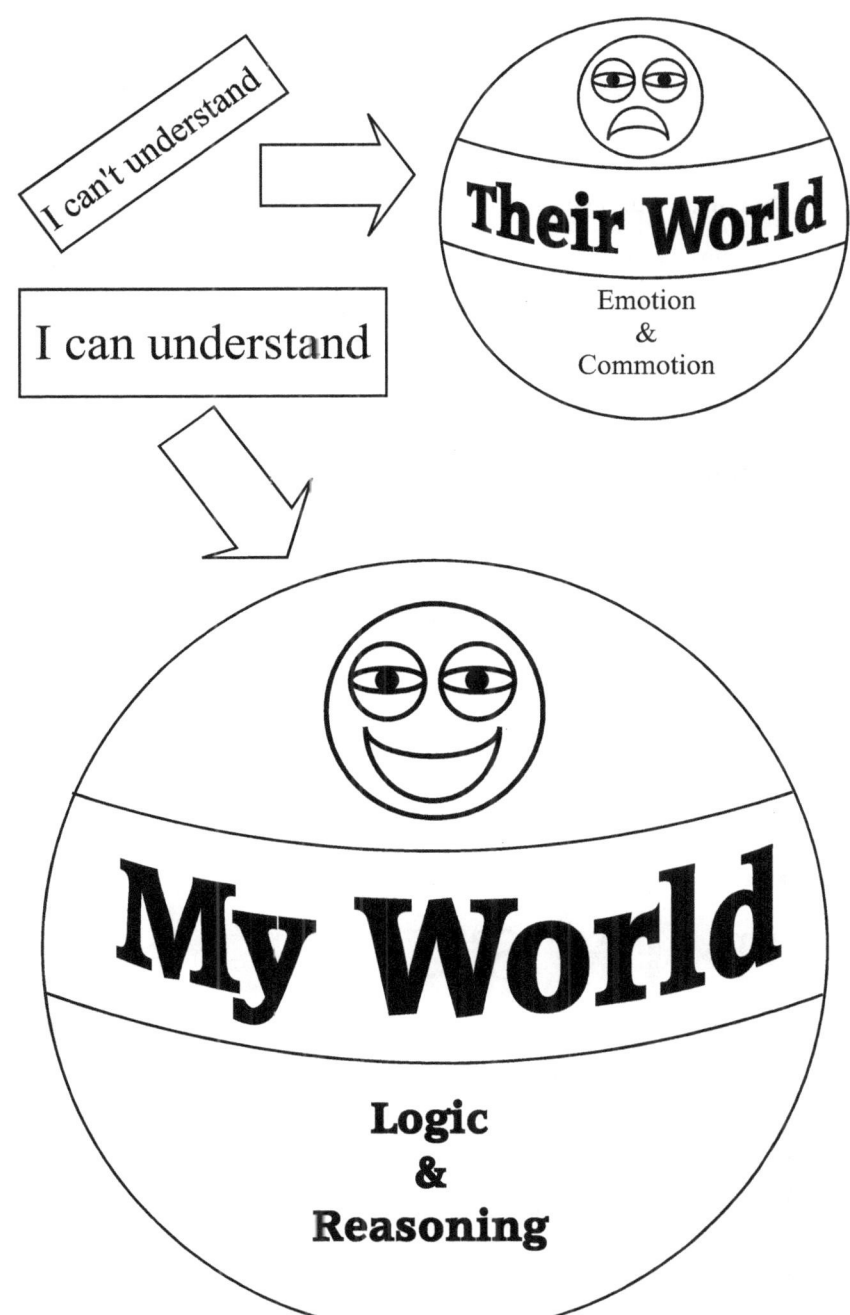

Section X
The After Math

Setting: The last educational (if you can call it that) class of the day and the horrormoaners are ready to go home. The Innocent Bystandards are bored stiff. They are longing for entertainment and are itchy for satisfaction.

Climax: Innocent Bystandards start questioning the horrormoaners on arbitrary subjects they don't understand and never will. The horrormoaners don't know what hit them and defensively offend.

Conclusion: Satisfaction guaranteed.

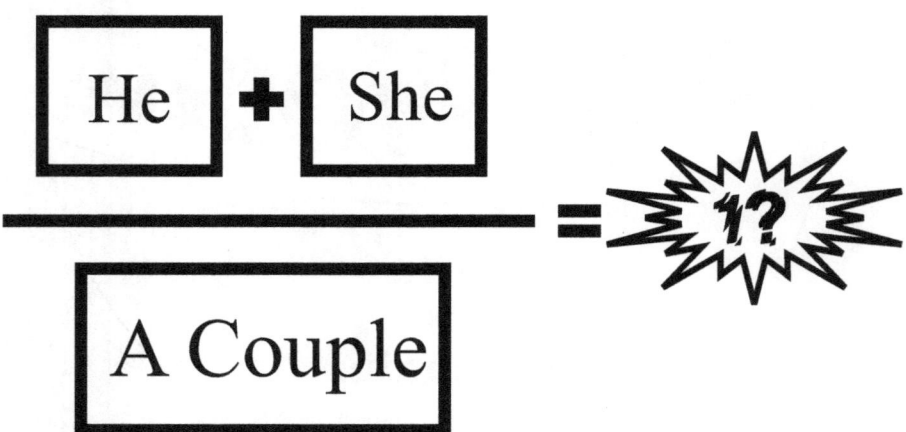

Comments

I was often bored in my classes. The material was way too easy, and I often remembered information after only hearing it once. I got impatient when teachers repeated things, and I blamed that on the other students' incompetence. This same boredom nearly forced me to quit school the next year. I needed a more challenging environment, where intellect was celebrated and being different was okay.

This was another case of understanding versus emotion. Here, I recognized that I had a far superior understanding of many (cerebral) things, and I believed that this put me way above the horrormoaners. But what I was unable to connect to, was the emotional pieces that the horrormoaners felt, and I thought that my understanding, that my intellect, was far superior to whatever they were doing or responding to.

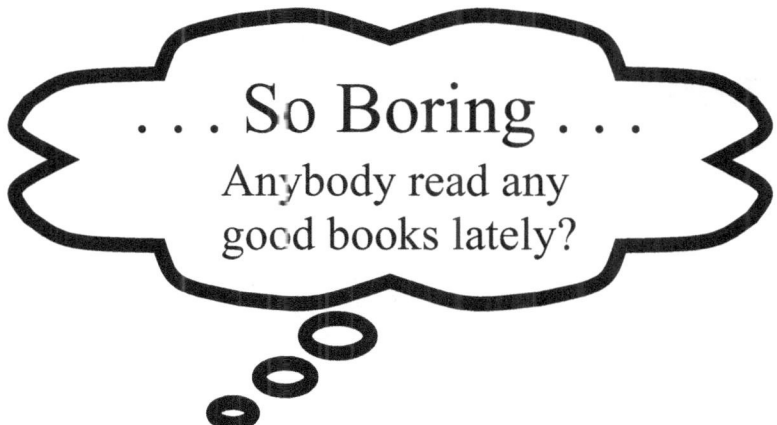

Section XI
Socially Studying

Setting: Horrormoaners are out of control! The Innocent Bystandards stand by and watch. Luckily at this point it's just eyes and words.

Climax: He finds out that she likes him, but he heard that his friends like her, who is now staring intently at—if not through another horrormoaner. Innocent Bystandard grows bored quick and pulls out something of worth to occupy their time*. The horrormoaner on the other hand, is out of focus and control = only with mental contacts right now**. Finally, he asks her out.

Conclusion: They go out for awhile, but it grows cold, so they come back in.

Right Hand   # Wrong Hand

Focus & Control   Control

Comments

*Pocket lint for example . . .

**"Only with mental contacts right now," means that the horrormoaner was in no way connected to what was going on around him, but only thinking about how to make the next move in a relationship.

To me, most of the time the other kids did seem to be out of control. And probably sometimes they were. If I tried to understand what was happening, I grew frustrated. Consequently, I ended up ignoring a lot of what was happening around me, which caused me to draw even more inside myself.

Again I enjoyed the word plays here. I really felt that the pocket lint was more interesting than anything they could possibly find to talk about.

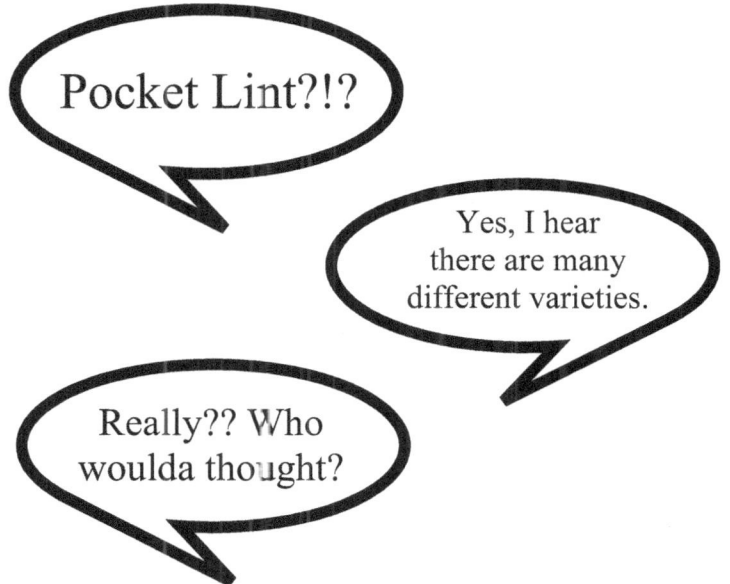

Section XII
The Art of Expression

Setting: Last period occupying a dull day to the Innocent Bystandard, watching observantly for some excitement. Horrormoaners have lost it. The male percentage of horrormoaners have their pants down around their ankles and are sucking in attention from wherest* it will come. The female percentile of horrormoaners on the other hand (or foot as the case may be), are wearing skirts going down to their waist.

Climax: Horrormoaners attention feed each other (apparently there was a deficit) until they are forced to comply with the dress code that was set up. Innocent Bystandard just ignores the whole situation. It was just a brief piece of the day that was unworthy to pay any attention to.

Conclusion: Innocent Bystandard becomes privately humiliated to even think about, or see such events taking place in public.

Comments

*wherest = wherever

    This is primarily in reference to when it became popular to begin wearing jeans down around the lower hips. I never understood why people paid so much attention to clothing, as I found it one of the most boring subjects on earth. I still do not get it. Although for them, it was a way to gain acceptance into the group, explore who they were, and interact socially, I felt it, "unworthy to pay any attention to."

    I am also making a few Freudian references here. I could not understand why in the world they would want to touch (or do other things to) each other. It did not make any sense at all to me, and I was completely mortified by the thought that kids my age were doing the things that I had seen them doing, especially all the touching. I just did not get it. And that was probably another reason I wanted them to just stay away from me.

    I also talk about the attention piece, because many of the kids I went to school with seemed unable to focus on anything important for more than a few seconds at a time. Little did I realize that they were so engrossed in so much other stuff (that was truly real to them), that there were often good reasons for their inability to focus.

However, this was not something I realized until I spent some time working as an educational technician in a middle school, at which point, I had finally gained enough language skills and life experience to be able to ask the kids what in the world they were doing!?!

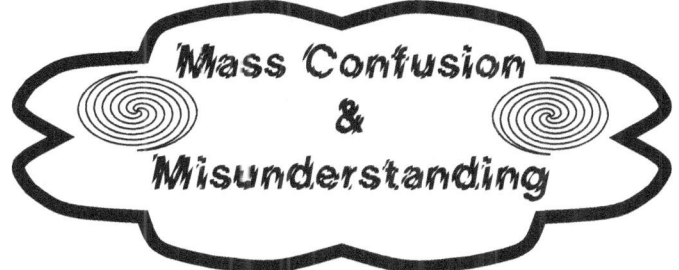

Section XIII
Bathroom Break

Setting: All of the horrormoaners find the dire need to visit the bathroom in between each and every class—or anything else going on. Innocent Bystandard has a personal problem, which can be taken care of in a responsible manner within a matter of a couple of minutes.

Climax: Innocent Bystandard heads casually into the bathroom to find only the lurking horrormoaners. Impossible to go about business, Innocent Bystandard quickly exits and makes the decision to find another bathroom. One is tracked down, but when Innocent Bystandard stepped in, they were stepped on by horrormoaners—this time in a cluster.

Conclusion: Innocent Bystandard, this time 100% caught in a jam, goes home, takes care of business, and falls asleep, having dreams about unappropriate* for school ordeals taking place in the bathroom.

Comments

*unappropriate = inappropriate

I absolutely HATED going to the bathroom at school, and would avoid it at all costs. I just thought it was because they were dirty, and I never really gave it much more thought than that. But part of it was that I never knew who was going to be in the bathroom at school. It would be a terrible place to run into someone I did not want to see. In addition, they were so noisy. I never ever went in between classes. I would always leave class to go if it was necessary, because there was less chance of other people being in there. And I would go find another bathroom (there were only three choices when I was in eighth grade) if there was too much going on in the one I had chosen.

I really feel like the last line, not only again addresses the piece of emotion vs. understanding, but it also touches on my sensory issues. I said that I went home and fell asleep. Home was a safe place to go and decompress. Sleeping was always what happened when I got overloaded sensory-wise. I never actually just wandered home and slept in the middle of the day (it was too far to walk!), but now I recognize that sometimes I needed to.

In addition, this also shows that I was sometimes completely grossed out by the other kids. Their out-of-control hormones and the things that they were doing just seemed so inappropriate and unbelievable. I could not even imagine what was going on with them to cause them to behave in what I viewed to be, such rude and disgusting ways. I realize this sounds like they were taking off their clothes for money and having sex in the hallways or something (and perhaps some of them were . . .), but I am not talking about that. I am talking about holding hands or a kiss on the cheek. I did not get why anyone would do this at all.

Section XIV
Power Placement Pleas

Setting: Innocent Bystandard has had enough of horrormoaners' idiocracy*. Deciding to gain extreme power fast from a higher source, Innocent Bystandard formulates a plan to put horrormoaners in their well deserved place (especially after the bathroom break).

Climax: Innocent Bystandard tricks horrormoaners into falling under their command. They are locked in and absolutely can't escape. They feel it unnecessary to follow rule by peers, but when they step out of line are promptly put back in place.

Conclusion: All horrormoaners end up writing reports on how they, with their un(intellectual, etc...) talk, will not ever again embarrass or humiliate openly an Innocent Bystandard.

I will not humiliate Inocent Bystandrad.
I will not humiliate Inocent Bystandrad.
I will not humiliate Inocent Bystandrad.
I will not humiliate Inocent Bystandrad.
I will not humiliate Inocent Bystandrad.
I will not humiliate Inocent Bystandrad.
I will not humiliate Inocent Bystandrad.
I will not humiliate Inocent Bystandrad.
I will not humiliate Inocent Bystandrad.
I will not humiliate Inocent Bystandrad.
I will not humiliate Inocent Bystandrad.
I will not humiliate Inocent Bystandrad.
I will not humiliate Inocent Bystandrad.
I will not humiliate Inocent Bystandrad.
I will not humiliate Inocent Bystandrad.

Comments

*idiocracy = idiocy

Still talking about the bathroom here. And still feeling frustrated. I just wanted them to behave, to be . . . predictable. In some of my fantasies, I was the one controlling everything, because this way I would know exactly what was going on, and there would be no strange unexpected surprises. This was an attempt to somehow reconcile their behavior with mine, to bring the two worlds together, or rather absorb them into my own. I had them writing reports, and I referred to their unintellectual talk, suggesting that their talk should only be intellectual. And that was how I felt.

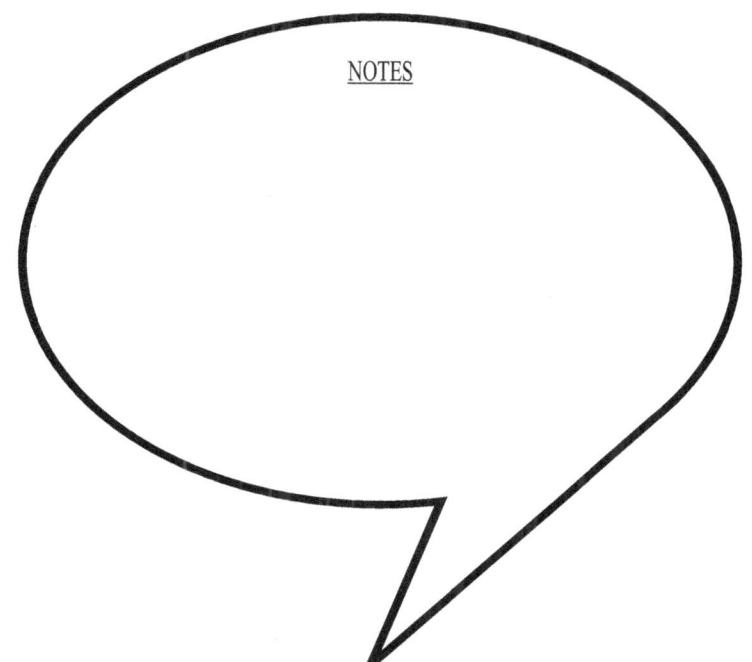

Section XV
Physical Education

Setting: First period, and the horrormoaners are all fired up and ready to shoot. Innocent Bystandards are pacing and conferring in their own groups about the day's business. They also have a vague idea as to what's going on with the horrormoaners . . . Unfortunately.

Climax: Horrormoaners feel it a needed asset* at this time to explain to each other that she likes him and he likes her and they like each other because he's got a great this and no one can beat her that.

Conclusion: Innocent Bystandard wakes up and hearing wind (about all it is) of what the horrormoaner said, decides to go back to sleep—not by their choice however.

Comments

*a needed asset = necessary

They always made references to each others' bodies, which I did not understand the reason for, and I also thought was gross. And they were always talking about who liked (and did not like) who, which I did not understand at all. None of it ever made any sense to me. And it made me want to curl up under some heavy blankets and go to sleep.

Section XVI
Busride Badgering

Setting: Horrormoaners are riproaring, and ready to instigate the millisecond they hopped on the bus that morning. Innocent Bystandard has not woken up yet.

Climax: Horrormoaners blatantly state (to each other, mind the reader) that he did this last night and she told him not to, but he didn't listen and just had to find out why he said that, when really it was her that said that he did that, and she was simply listening. She also can't wait to talk to her today because she said that she would ask him and she would tell him to tell her, who'd then tell her to tell him how it should work.

Conclusion: Innocent Bystandard is bored even more by these ongoing milestones* that they fall into a deeper sleep.

Comments

*"Milestones" refers to all the seemingly important (to the horrormoaners) events going on in the horrormoaners' lives.

The Innocent Bystandard here was still sleeping from the previous story. The bus was always a crowded noisy place, and it was basically all the people who drove me crazy at school packed into one tiny place. Sometimes I dealt with it the same way I did in the classroom. I made conversation with one of my only allies, the bus driver. Other times I dove into my studies and focused on my homework (I made it a policy to never do homework at home). And other times I just escaped into my own world and stared out the window.

Luckily, I enjoyed riding. I found the motion to be relaxing, and watching things out the window intriguing. Sometimes I looked at nothing, and other times I counted telephone poles. Sometimes I just watched people. Staying inside myself was much less confusing and much more peaceful than whatever was going on in the world around me.

Also, the way the Climax is written here is really what this type of talk sounds like to me. I am still rather unable to process it. It just does not connect.

Section XVII
Cafeteria Crisis

Setting: There are no Innocent Bystandards within at least a good 50 foot radius. Horrormoaners are complaining at and about each other to each other. The decibel level is close to a record.

Climax: Lunch is received by those who accepted the generous gift given to them by the wonderful cooks. Though one may only assume what is in the food. Now, most accepted the food. No one however, wished to eat it. So he threw it at her because he thought she threw it at him. But, he missed and hit them. They turned and flung it at another cluster of them, but missed and hit her.

Conclusion: Horrormoaners stay after school cleaning the cafeteria spotless, while Innocent Bystandard can only laugh.

Comments

Another sensory piece, "the decibel level is close to a record." They were so noisy. All the time. And even just thinking about it now makes me feel irritated.

I hated going into the cafeteria, even to get my lunch. They did have food fights, and that did not make any sense to me either. Why would anyone want to throw food? It is for eating.

I am unable to eat if there is a lot of noise around me or if there is something in the environment that disturbs me (and this could be anything . . . bright lights or an ugly picture on the wall. And sometimes I do not know what it is . . . but noise is the worst). I get anxious and irritated and I just want to go into my bedroom and hide under my covers. I was lucky to be able to eat every day in a quiet classroom from sixth grade all the way up through high school.

Section XVIII
Toe Jammed Teacher

Setting: Horrormoaners are doing what they do best before class. They didn't seem to realize it wasn't okay for them to continue their conversation. Innocent Bystandard offered them a mouth full of toe jam. They refused and were quiet for ten seconds.

Climax: Innocent Bystandard decides to teach them a lesson. Pulling all the toe lint together that he has access to, he places it within the snacks of the horrormoaners.

Conclusion: All horrormoaners are sick with Tomaine* poisoning. There is somewhat peace at school between the eighth graders.

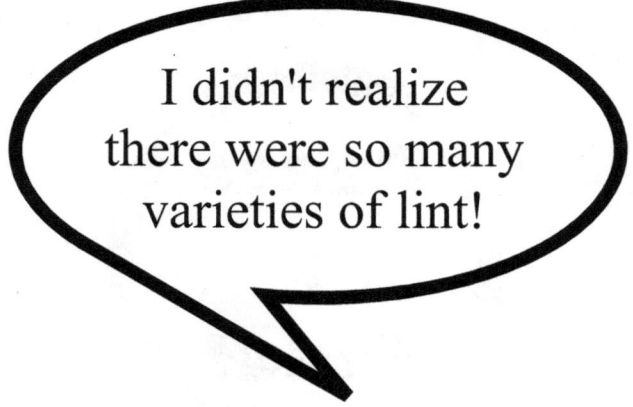

Comments

*Tomaine = Ptomaine

Of course, I never actually acted on this fantasy. It is pretty disgusting. But I was disgusted with the way they were behaving too, and I was always trying to think of ways to either teach them a lesson or to make them behave better.

Sometimes I just wished they would go away. I never wished them any harm, but I just wished they would leave me alone, leave me to my own world and stop flooding me with all their crazy emotions. They drove me nuts, and yet somewhere inside I wished I was a part of their group. Even the few friends I had left were able to interact with them on some level, whereas I was completely deficient.

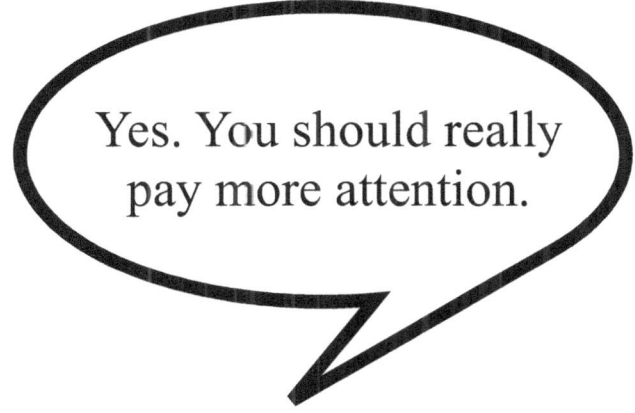

Section XIX
What Work?

Setting: Horrormoaners are actually quite content today (must be the weather). They still of course have their prime focus on one another. Now, this particular group of horrormoaners are not at all auditory or multi-modal [learners]. They are extremely visual or hands on. Somehow, Innocent Bystandards are able to converse intelligently among themselves without being disturbed by them.

Climax: At the end of the period, all students are asked to hand in their 3-week projects. All Innocent Bystandards (and others—not important to plot) stand and proceed to pass in their reports. Horrormoaners complain they were never told of the assignment.

Conclusion: Horrormoaners are now officially beyond repair and are told to go home.

Comments

This happened often. Assignment due. Lots of time to work on it in class. And still, some kids never even bothered to start. What were they doing?!? I recognized that their prime focus was one another, but what I did not know was WHY? I was more focused (as were the teachers) on why they could not get their homework done. I really did not understand why, when they had such a simple assignment with so much time, that they could not get it done. I did not realize how much else goes on in kids' lives until I worked as an educational technician in a middle school.

Then I began to see how homework could take a back seat. But at the time, for all intents and purposes, those kids were useless and an obstruction to my learning. Ironically, now I see them as my teachers.

Section XX
Relatively Speaking

Setting: Horrormoaners tend to "grade each other on a curve" and may turn on each other at any given time. Innocent Bystandards don't even bother to pay attention to this infantile eighth grade behavior.

Climax: Not worth mentioning.

Conclusion: It's 2:30 and time to go home.

Comments

Infantile eighth grade behavior. That is all I knew. That is what I saw all day long, and I was happy every day when I could leave it behind.

Section XXI
Rapid Redundancy

Setting: Horrormoaners are in the classroom awaiting the already given instructions. They have already been given instructions a number of times and still don't know what to do. Innocent Bystandard becomes annoyed and tunes out the corny behavior exhibited by them.

Climax: Innocent Bystandard has extremely low tolerance for idiots today and decides to make an announcement. Taking the responsibility upon themselves they rise with a prideful stride forward calling attention to their plea.

Conclusion: After a matter of seconds, Innocent Bystandard gives up and goes into hiding.

NOTES

Comments

Not only do I hate hearing things over and over again, but I hate hearing them more than once, which may seem ironic for as much as I clarify and reword in my writing. I absolutely hated redundancy then, and I blamed most of it on the kids who did not know how to listen to instructions, but only knew how to fool around with each other. Because of them, I had to endure the redundancy.

This was perhaps the type of thing I wished I had the confidence to do at the time. There were many things I wanted to tell them, most of which would have entailed telling them to go away. But in the end, as here, I never said much at all. Although one time, one of them came up to me and put his arm around my shoulder. I was not expecting it, and had no idea what he was doing. Then something happened, and I threw him across the room. He never touched me again, and I do not think anybody else in the class ever did either. But why was he touching me in the first place?!? It made no sense! And even now when I think about it, I feel just as perplexed as I did then!

Section XXII
Personal Problems

Setting: Horrormoaners are at it once again. They feel it necessary to exhibit every piece of their raw, living being because of the attention disorder going on. Innocent Bystandard just watches the battle for attention take place (and tries to remember it's just that).

Climax: The horrormoaners have gone just plain too far this time for the Innocent Bystandards. They have decided to let everyone see the color, style, price and all other information about their under attire by wearing the under attire on the outside attire, making the under attire, over attire.

Conclusion: Innocent Bystandard hides all day behind a wall.

Comments

It became a well-known joke among the small circle of people who I could tolerate that I became extremely embarrassed at the mention of underwear or any similar topic. There was one girl who loved purple, and one day, she was talking about matching her underwear with her clothes. I do not know why anybody would want to match their underwear with their clothes or even think that much about underwear.

It has always been an extremely embarrassing topic for me. I remember my resistance to beginning to wear bras. When it got to the point that I really needed one, in fifth grade, I began by wearing a bathing suit because that was something familiar. Then I switched over to a sports bra. I was too embarrassed to think about, let alone try the other kind of bra, and I did not want to wear anything that looked like that, let alone go and look for anything that looked like that. Also, I did not like the feeling of the material that most regular bras were made of. It felt abrasive to me.

Unfortunately for me, some of my family members also love to talk about underwear and bras. You can imagine my embarrassment when we went shopping one day, and one of them shouted into the store, "Jessica, are we gonna get you a new bra today?" I was mortified. So this passage is in reference to those feelings.

I also have a lot of issues with clothing, including always wanting to wear familiar clothes (for which I am very particular about material, fit, etc.), along with difficulty buying or wearing new clothing without wanting to replace my whole wardrobe. This is because I feel uncomfortable wearing new and old clothing at the same time.

Hiding Behind a Wall . . .

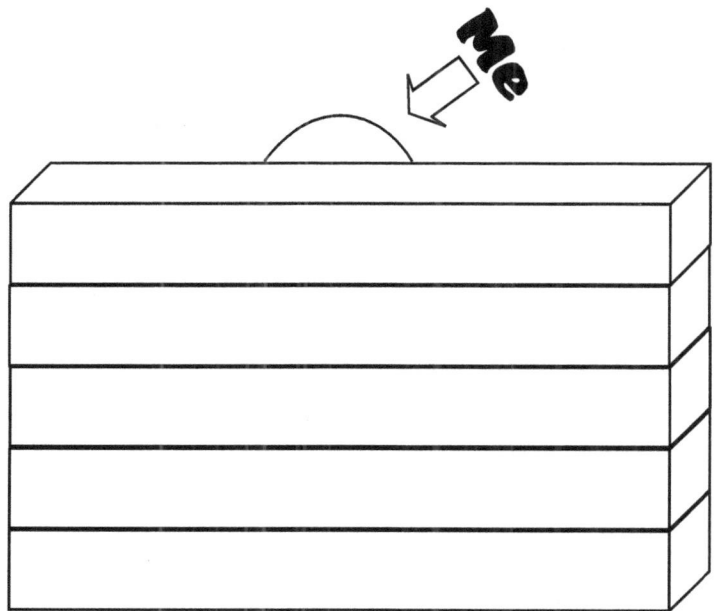

Section XXIII
Trivial Complaints

Setting: Horrormoaners have become annoyed with the Innocent Bystandards, for their intellect and wit. Though they know not of what these things are, they have recognized they are missing something.

Climax: Horrormoaners try to get back at the Innocent Bystandards by telling on them for every smart move they make. Finally, some entertainment for the Innocent Bystandards. They find it utterly enjoyable.

Conclusion: The complaints soon cease and they return back to their abnormal selves (though they feel normal).

Comments

I always thought that the other kids did not like me because I was too smart. And I thought that this was the reason we did not get along well with each other. Although it was me, at the time, I thought it was they who were deficient. I thought it was they who were missing the intellect. I never suspected it might be me who was missing the emotion.

Section XXIV
Instant Gratification

Setting: Horrormoaners are arbitrary in this section. SeeMeHearMe however, is not. SeeMeHearMe finishes work and feels the need to have their work evaluated right away. Innocent Bystandard regards this as normal SeeMeHearMe behavior and pays little attention.

Climax: SeeMeHearMe has been trying to gain attention while being fully ignored by peers and those of the older persuasion*. They have some sort of hyperactive bone in them and are soon going to destruct. Their attention is granted so they cool down.

Conclusion: SeeMeHearMes become ban** from school and other public facilities unless they find somewhere else to gain attention.

Comments

*"Those of the older persuasion," refers to teachers and other adults.
**ban = banned

The SeeMeHearMes drove me nuts. They were generally loud and obnoxious, and I did not do well in the same room with them, since I liked things calm and quiet. These kids were often the ones with the focus issues, and usually the ones who could not manage to do their homework at all, let alone on time. However, when they did complete something, they wanted the teacher's immediate attention. It did not matter what else was going on. And that also drove me nuts. In this passage, I am expressing that frustration.

Section XXV
Going Home Economically

Setting: Horrormoaners are awful today. So bad, they are driving the Innocent Bystandard crazy. Innocent Bystandard needs to plot a plan.

Climax: Innocent Bystandard offers horrormoaner a paid trip to their homeland of Testosterhome. Innocent Bystandard offers bits of fake information as to who's going out with who and when. They agree.

Conclusion: Testosterhome gives them encouragement and sends them back to the Innocent Bystandard.

Comments

Some days were more difficult than others. I always wanted to send the people who were bothering me away. In this story, I created a plan to do so.

Creating plans is something I do very well. It is something I have done as far back as I can remember in order to create a sense of order where there does not seem to be any. Plans help me feel safe, and they are essentially what have helped me function and get to the place I am now. The problems occur when things do not happen according to the plans in my head.

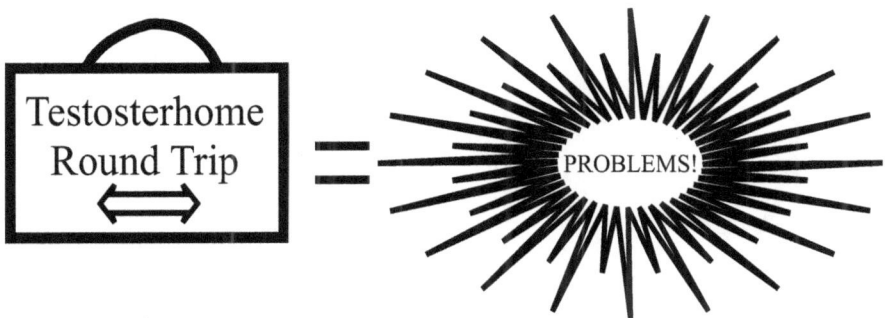

Section XXVI
Keying in on Bored Cells

Setting: Horrormoaners are hitting hard today. After their visit to Testosterhome, they have gone wild. They are racing. All Innocent Bystandards can do is stand by and watch.

Climax: Horrormoaners are playing touchy feely eye to eye and Innocent Bystandards rapidly* ignore the trauma of it all.

Conclusion: Innocent Bystandards find petty amusement in the stupidity of it all.

Comments

*rapidly = are trying hard to

Trauma is actually a very good way to describe what I was experiencing. I really did not know what was going on around me. I had lost most of my friends, and I was unable to successfully form new relationships. I continued to be dependent on my mother, and cling to those who took care of me with a death grip. I was losing everyone I had known growing up, and I was so scared I was going to lose the people I really cared about, such as my family. Over and over again we talked about death, which became one of my obsessions. And over and over again, the people who took care of me continued to be there for me.

Section XXVII
Rough Drifts are Due Tomorrow

Setting: Horrormoaners are focused primarily on the SeeMe-HearMes. The SeeMeHearMe behavior is socially unacceptable (well, more than usual). For some reason, they feel compelled to not only hover today, but to actually make contact. Horrormoaners are rather surprised, yet don't show it. They just try to put the SeeMeHearMes back in their place.

Climax: SeeMeHearMe is rimracking* horrormoaners, Innocent Bystandards, and other mass that hasn't been mentioned yet. Innocent Bystandard decided word plays won't work for reasons that SeeMeHearMe won't understand anyway. Horrormoaners attention feed, trying to put them in the state where they feel they belong**. They're beyond listening though. They always were.

Conclusion: Next day everything is back to the primitive form of communication abuse***.

Comments

*rimrack = bother. This is a word I made up.

**Horrormoaners gave SeeMeHearMes attention, trying to make them happy.

***"Primitive form of communication abuse," means what I perceived to be the primitive way in which the horrormoaners communicated with each other. They did not know how to play with language, and the things they did say (usually emotionally charged) did not make any sense to me. Since they could not use the language properly (in my opinion), I felt this was a kind of abuse of language.

It is interesting that I labeled the behavior of the more social kids as socially unacceptable, when in fact my behavior could hardly have been considered social at all. My solution to the touchy-feelyness was to use intellect, wit, word plays, and to go into hiding, mainly because I did not know what else to do. Most of what I tried to communicate was missed by all but a couple of people who knew me well.

It is also interesting that I refer to what my peers were doing as a primitive form of communication. That is how it appeared to me. Developed forms of communication should use words, I reasoned. And yet, they were functioning almost solely from their emotions. In any case, their behavior, not mine, was likely developmentally very appropriate.

Section XXVIII
Intellectual Inequalities

Setting: This story goes without saying, but for the record, it shall be said! Horrormoaners are putting down everything and anything that gets in their way. SeeMeHearMes see nothing new, while Innocent Bystandard sees opportunities.

Climax: Innocent Bystandard sees horrormoaners' unhealthy state and like a virus goes in for the attack (getting on the offense). Horrormoaner is properly placed face down where they belong (not in a violent manner, of course). SeeMeHearMe pays no attention whatsoever.

Conclusion: Horrormoaners moan amongst themselves over Innocent Bystandard's victory.

Comments

I was searching for acceptance, and I really wanted to be okay. At this point, the only way I really knew how to interact was to dominate, and that is what this story is about.

One example is a debate we did in the eighth grade. I practically did the whole debate myself, without even letting my opponent speak. I brought up new topics, gave reasons, and brought up counter arguments to my own opinion in order to refute them. I remember the poor boy's face who I was "debating against" He just sat there dumbfounded, which was pretty rare for a SeeMeHearMe horrormoaner. I felt a sense of victory because for once he was finally quiet.

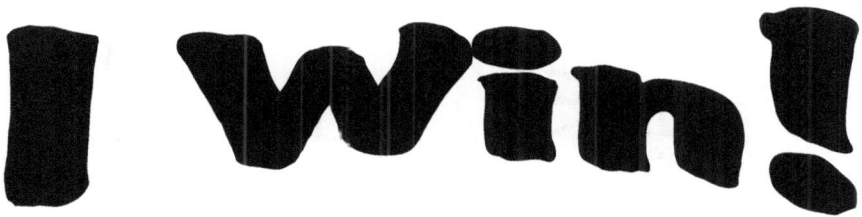

Section XXIX
Petrifying Predicaments

Setting: Horrormoaner's hair is misbehaving (or so they think). Innocent Bystandard is once again at locker* doing a book exchange.

Climax: Horrormoaners are clumped up at (supposedly at the locker next to), and on the Innocent Bystandard's locker. The deadly hairspray can is revealed; A deadly weapon. Attack! The Innocent Bystandard is rapidly diminishing** through this environmental hazard.

Conclusion: Innocent Bystandard is sick in bed for the next two days because the ozone killers hit hard.

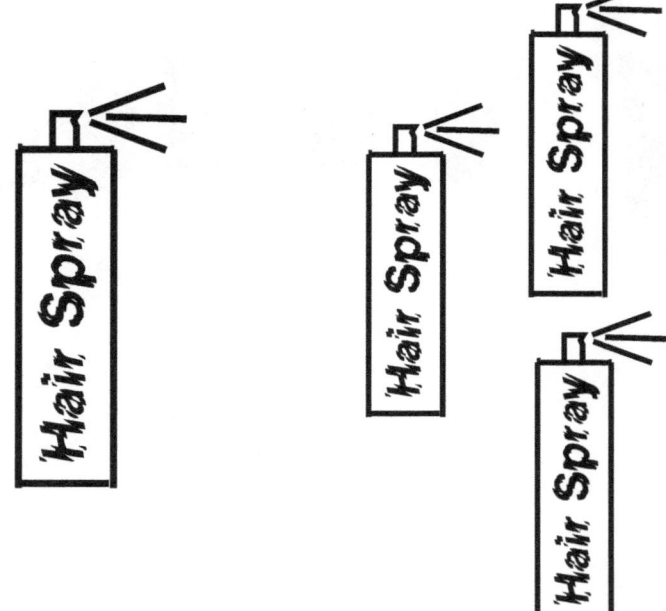

Comments

*Innocent Bystandard's locker (to get books between classes)
**diminishing = deteriorating

Most of the kids, especially the girls, were often concerned about their hair. I was never concerned about hair, as I had always worn the same style since I was a child, a long braid.

I did not care much about hair, but I was concerned about books, in this case getting them so I would not be late for my next class, which I also worried about obsessively. Then, I became concerned about people spraying hairspray. I hate hairspray. It not only smells bad, but it overwhelms my senses, and I just hate it. And I really used to get angry when they would spray it at school in the hallways or in the bathroom because I could smell it throughout the school. Often I would carry around seven classes worth of books to avoid going to my locker during the day. Smell is a major sensory issue for me. I have become dysfunctional a number of times when the scents around me were overwhelming.

At the end of this story, I am in bed (proverbially) for two whole days because of the sensory overload, although I did not have a name for it at the time.

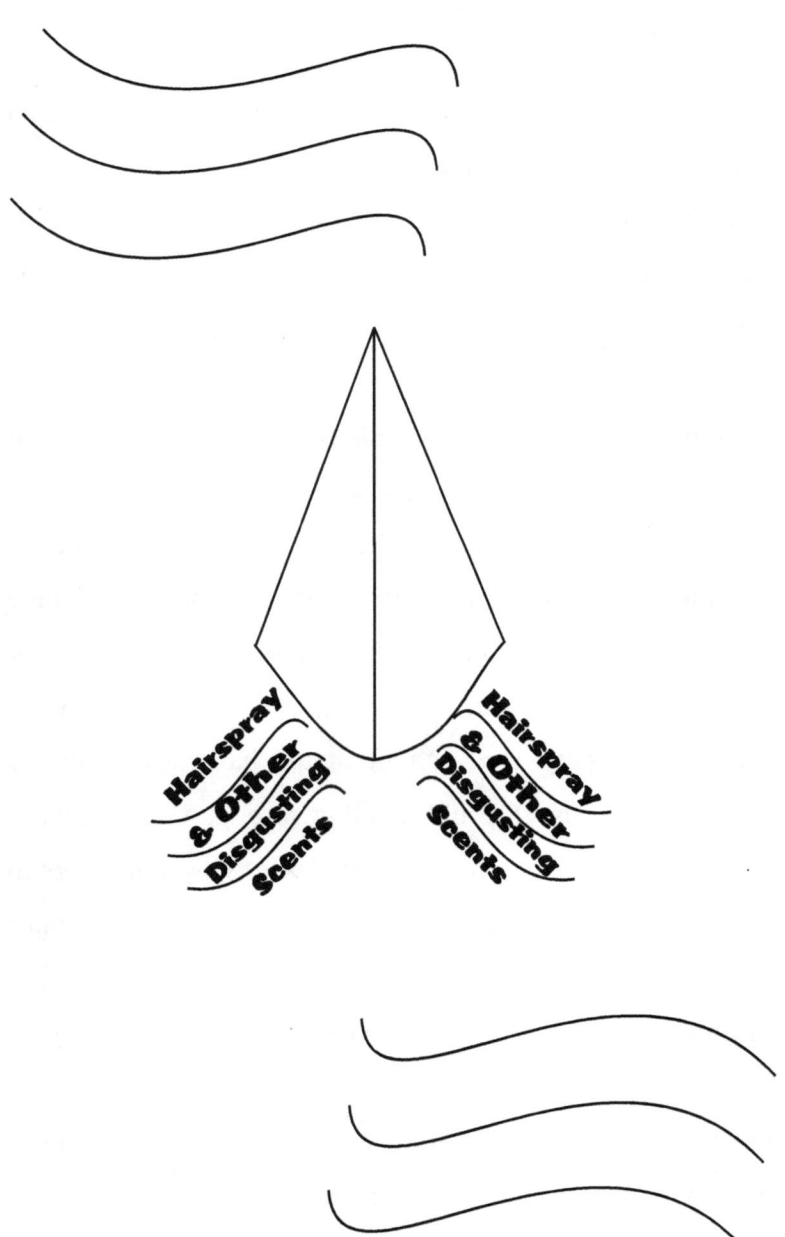

Section XXX

Arbitrary Annihilation

Setting: Innocent Bystandards are fired up and ready to pay back all the horrormoaners for the trouble of a few. SeeMe-HearMes just need to stay out of the way—not a probable plea*.

Climax: Bang! First period. Horrormoaner is nailed by Innocent Bystandard for cheating. Second period—same offense (so they're redundant buggers). Throughout the rest of the day, it is sheer humiliation and torture for the horrormoaners.

Conclusion: Horrormoaners are cranky and go home complaining.

Comments

*not a probable plea = not likely

 I was always so angry at the behaviors of the other kids. I did not understand them at all. And I was always trying to look for ways to get them in trouble or to show them that they were not doing the best they could. And it did not make sense to me, because many of the kids were smart. They just did not act it. They acted like hormone-ridden teenagers.

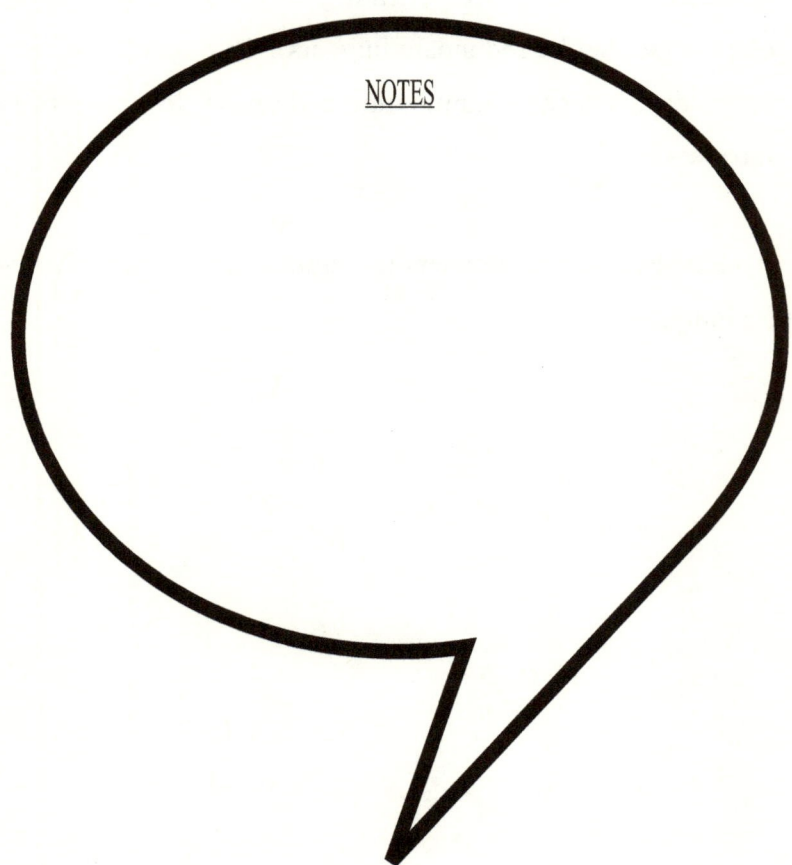

Section XXXI
A Notable Falling

Setting: Innocent Bystandard intently watches (though not too intently) the SeeMeHearMes roll in. Horrormoaners then slide in late.

Climax: Demerit day again! Sale . . . 3 for 1 at the Issuer's par. The Issuers are looking to nail the horrormoaners and possibly SeeMeHearMes today (it is rather impossible to nail Innocent Bystandards, for all they do is stand and observe).

Conclusion: All horrormoaners and SeeMeHearMes are suspended . . . Forever.

Comments

I wish . . . then I would not have been so overwhelmed by them. However, there was no indefinite suspension for anyone. Some days though, the teachers would look for kids to give demerits to. They would also tell them that the amount would be doubled or tripled in certain cases. The kids did not pay much attention, and I was happy because I figured they were that much closer to being out of my hair.

Incidentally, I did not even group myself with the other kids. I was not concerned about the teachers giving me demerits, as I felt that I was a part of them. All throughout middle school, I received threats from numerous teachers, but only one teacher ever acted on it, and she was not my friend.

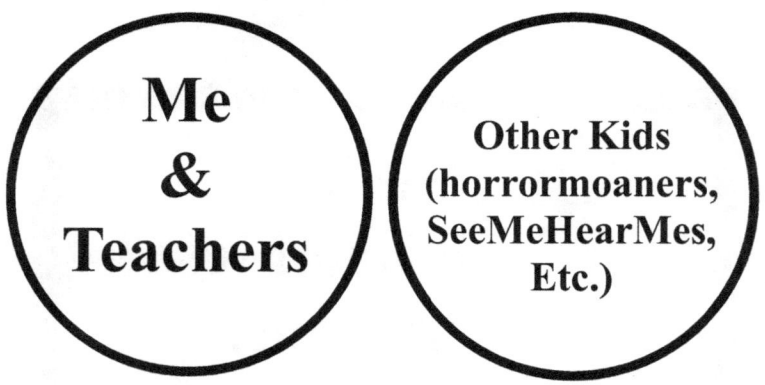

Long Distance Horrormoaners

Long Distance Horrormoaners

Long Distance Horrormoaners is a collection of stories based on the experiences I had when a childhood friend, who had moved away when I was quite young, came back to visit school with me for the day. She wanted to see all of our old friends again. I was mortified by her behavior, which I considered to be completely out of control, but which was no different than the other kids our age. The teachers were growing angry and irritated with her behavior in the same way they had with the other kids. And because she was technically my responsibility, I felt that the only people who had been my allies, the teachers, were beginning to turn against me. It was an awful feeling. And I did not know what to do. So I have written about my experiences here.

As a note, I think when the teachers read these stories, they could see that I felt the whole thing was as ridiculous as they did.

Section I	Phone Fright I
Section II	House Harousing
Section III	Busride Blues
Section IV	Morning Madness
Section V	Hallway Hubbub

Section VI	Classroom Route Canals
Section VII	Outside Indentures
Section VIII	Crafty Chaos
Section IX	Lunch Lagoon
Section X	Battle Through the Break
Section XI	Math Stemulants
Section XII	Homeroom Horrormoaning
Section XIII	Promotional PMS
Section XIV	Tearable Report
Section XV	Oh Boy!
Section XVI	Clothes Call!
Section XVII	New News
Section XVIII	Avoiding Avengers
Section XIX	Phone Fright II

Section I
Phone Fright I

Setting: Innocent Bystandard is tolerating the awaited (presently happening) phone call by unexpected horrormoaner. Horrormoaner is enjoying the enlightening conversation while Innocent Bystandard sweats it out.

Climax: Horrormoaner wants to know if they are able to participate in school for a day with Innocent Bystandard. Innocent Bystandard, who as a weakness, can't say no, says yes with about as much enthusiasm as a rock.

Conclusion: Innocent Bystandard feels that maybe it won't be all that bad and goes to bed.

Comments

This was a good friend who had moved away when I was in elementary school. We had known each other since kindergarten, and our mothers were friends. When I got the news that she was coming back to visit for a couple of days, naturally I was happy. When I do make a close friend, I consider them my close friend for life. She was going to call me, and I was all excited.

Then something unexpected happened. She called me, and during the course of the phone call, I realized that she was not the same person I had once known. In fact, she was someone I did not know at all, and was acting like most of the kids at school, whose strange behavior perplexed me daily. She was asking me strange questions, like if there were any cute boys, and what people looked like. The answers to both of which I had no idea.

I did not want to bring her to school with me. In fact, I now hated having to bring her. But what else could I do?

Section II

House Harousing

Setting: Innocent Bystandard is unanxiously awaiting the horrormoaner's arrival. Horrormoaner unfinally arrives wearing oversized clashing clothes.

Climax: Horrormoaner interrupts necessary chores taking place in the morning. Innocent Bystandard, from this horrible moment on, knows that the rest of the day will be nothing but pure torture.

Conclusion: Innocent Bystandard is made to drag horrormoaner to school only to be exhausted.

Comments

I remember when she showed up at my house. It still makes me feel sick to my stomach. She was wearing oversized black bell bottom pants, and a shirt with colors that even I could tell did not match. Morning was always crazy at my house anyway since there were so many of us getting ready for school, and when the routine got disrupted, it made things even more difficult. When any of my routines gets disrupted it makes life difficult, but especially when I know that what follows is not only going to be unexpected, but likely unpleasant.

NOTES

Section III
Busride Blues

Setting: Innocent Bystandard trudges onto the morning bus as horrormoaner lurks on.

Climax: Innocent Bystandard is bashed by unteen* million questions concerning primarily the male persuasion and every now and then a question of what sort of industrial practice** had taken place over the last however many years.

Conclusion: Innocent Bystandard is mulling over what the unfortunate rest of the day holds for them.

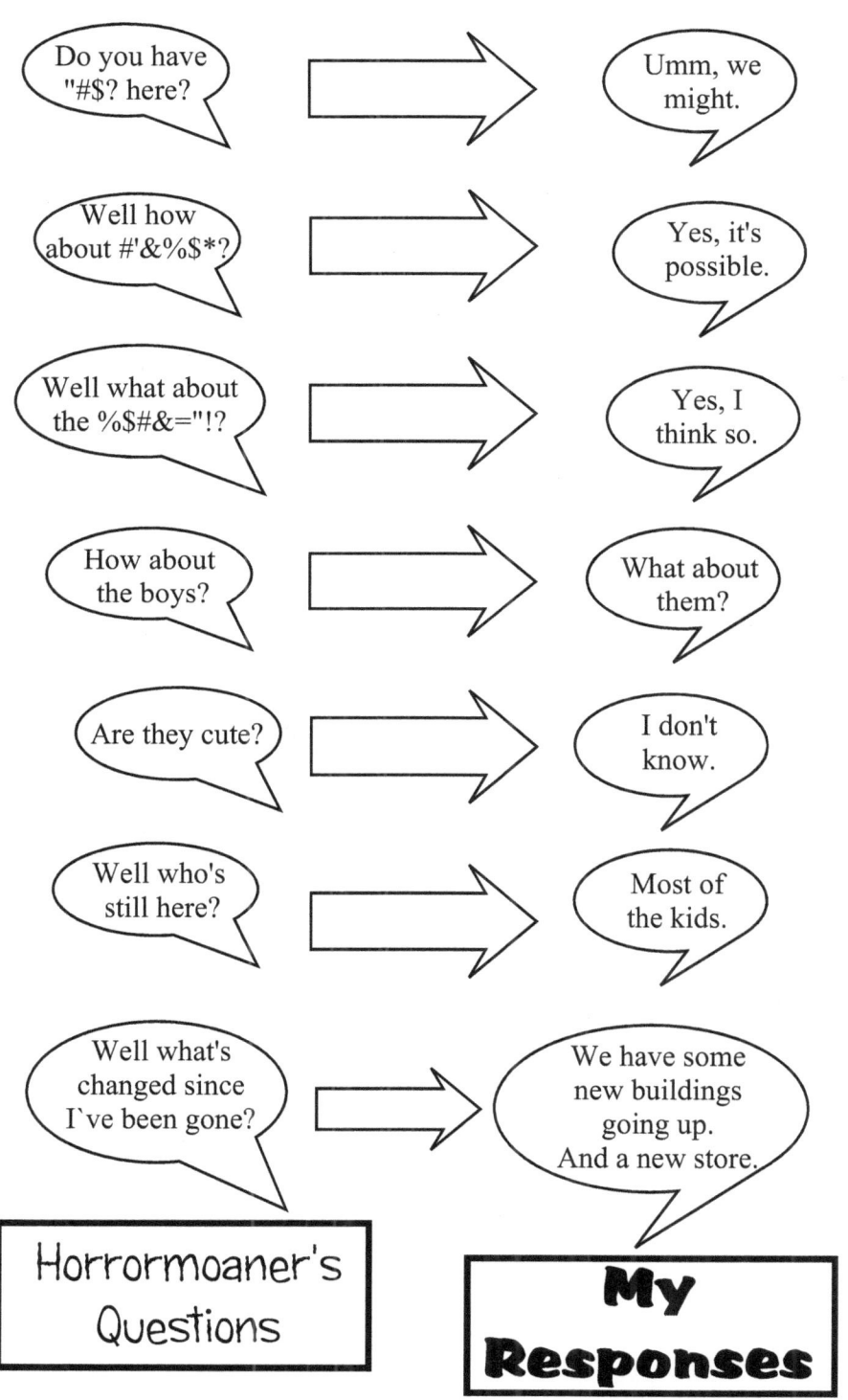

Comments

*unteen = umpteen

**". . . question of what sort of industrial practice," means questions about the changes in the town.

I took her with me on the bus, but I did not want to. Of course things had changed since she had left, but she was not interested in the kinds of changes I was willing to talk about. I did not mind talking about who had built a house or who had moved away. She wanted to talk about the guys at school, which not only did I not have any interest in talking about, and was even embarrassed and disgusted to talk about, but I did not know how to talk about. She was asking questions for which I had no reference point, and I do not even remember what they were, because they seemed so strange and obscure.

I was so scared about what was going to happen when we got to school. And as it turned out, my fears were warranted.

Section IV
Morning Madness

Setting: Innocent Bystandard drags horrormoaner through uncivilized morning commotion consisting of the usual practices.

Climax: Horrormoaner, for about the only time during anytime withdraws—though still being questioned by all. Innocent Bystandard tries to stay in own world and never wishes to exit.

Conclusion: Innocent Bystandard is prodded by higher control units as to the contents of the day with the wonderful new discovery.

Comments

She was a bit shy when we arrived, as the morning cafeteria with about fifteen billion screaming kids could be a bit overwhelming for anybody.

I liked to keep to myself. I understood my own world, but I did not understand the world that was happening outside. My own world was a safe place, and in fact, I made comments for years, starting around the eighth grade, that I wanted to go live in a forest somewhere (so that I did not have to deal with the world).

We had to go to the office to sign her in, and the secretaries and the principal were the "higher control units," who were asking me questions about the day . . . and likely telling me to keep her on a leash.

Section V
Hallway Hubbub

Setting: Long Distance moaner stirs up commotions in the hallway of another place just as well (if not better) than do the regular inhabitants. Innocent Bystandard is still trying to ignore the whole situation.

Climax: Horrormoaner pulls in attention at a tremendous rate (creating a deficit for the rest of the population to handle). Innocent Bystandard has had enough attention for one millennium and is having an overload and breakdown fast, embarrassed by the sort of weakness engulfing them. All the horrormoaner usuals are wound tighter than a top.

Conclusion: Innocent Bystandard pushes on as the awful-so-far day grows even worse.

Comments

As one can imagine, her coming drew a lot of attention from the kids, so much so in fact, that they had a more difficult time than usual paying attention. It is interesting when I look back at the kids now. They seemed like monsters to me, creatures I did not understand. But they can not be any worse than the middle schoolers today and I do not think they are monsters, but I am just beginning to understand them, and why they do the things they do.

I was mortified. I wanted to just pretend the whole thing, whatever indeed the whole thing was, was not happening. I wanted to crawl into a hole and hide for the day. The experience was so sensory overloading, that I really was having an emotional breakdown. Not to mention I was extremely embarrassed by what was happening, whatever exactly that was.

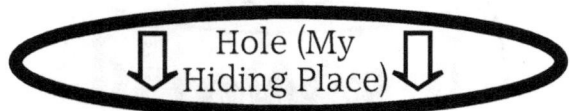

Section VI
Classroom Route Canals

Setting: Innocent Bystandard rushes off to class while horrormoaner of the away category, lags behind slowly (Though typical horrormoaner behavior, Innocent Bystandard can't and won't understand).

Climax: Now in class, horrormoaners moan among themselves, and not forgetting to include the newcomer, they do their usual thing. Innocent Bystandard uses this opportunity to accomplish something of use—though still intently watching Long Distance moaner for fear of escape.

Conclusion: Innocent Bystandard will do just about anything for a break—even give some sort of public lecture on unappropriate* for school issues, such as under attire.

Comments

*unappropriate = inappropriate

By this point, I was ready to do just about anything to be rid of the situation. I had had all I could take, and resigned to keep an eye on my "friend" (whom I was responsible for according to the school rules), from a distance. I was not going to allow her to make me late for class, and I just decided to do my own thing. I had work to do, and I could not let what was going on around me prevent me from getting it done.

Watching her took so much energy. In a way, it was good that she had the attention of all the other kids because that gave me a chance to study and get some work done. I always felt that if I had not studied enough during the day, that I was completely useless, unproductive, and lazy, a few of the worst things in my world.

Section VII
Outside Indentures

Setting: Innocent Bystandard zooms off to the next destination of the day while Horrormoaner, to be redundant, lags again.

Climax: Innocent Bystandard gets a break because a SeeMe-HearMe horrormoaner takes the Long Distance horrormoaner (also a SeeMeHearMe horrormoaner) outside. Innocent Bystandard is overjoyed.

Conclusion: Highlight of Innocent Bystandard's day so far is the conversation with another being of* unappropriate** for school issues.

Comments

* of = about

** unappropriate = inappropriate

I was thrilled when someone took her off my hands. Finally I could rest a bit.

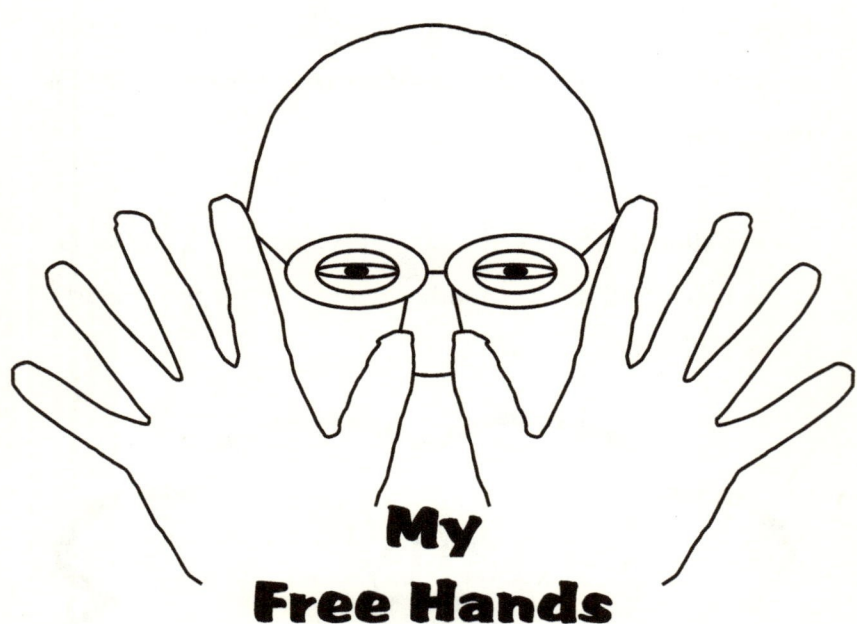

Section VIII
Crafty Chaos

Setting: All horrormoaners are ready to pop. Coming in from the outdoors has them out of control (now they are at a medium with their horrormoans)*. Innocent Bystandard ditches the horrormoaners for something more educationally stimulating taking place in another sector.

Climax: Long Distance moaner, without the needed supervision of Innocent Bystandard, does a wonderful job of sharing attention with all the other common horrormoaners. The exchange isn't at all practical, yet it's what's to be expected from where it's emulating** from.

Conclusion: Babysitter gives the Innocent Bystandard quite an earful when they return from their well established*** vacation. Innocent Bystandard promptly finds the lost attacker****.

Comments

*"At a medium with their horrormoans," means that their horrormoans were controlling their every action and decision.

**emulating = emanating

***established = earned

****"... the lost attacker," refers to my horrormoaner friend.

I had left her with Mr. Creature and a group of kids, and had gone to visit Ms. Doppler to calm down a bit. Mr. Creature seemed to be upset with me when I came back, and I did not understand his reaction, and moreover why he was blaming me. I could not control her any better than he could control the other kids. I was really angry at her for ruining my day.

NOTES

Section IX
Lunch Lagoon

Setting: Horrormoaner separates from Innocent Bystandard in the lunchroom upstairs for no apparent reason, leaving a piece of trash reading* (so-called) behind.

Climax: Lunch is accumulated through the Innocent Bystandard's digestive system during the lunch hour. (Horrormoaners incidentally, don't eat with Long Distance moaner at Lunch.) The Long Distance moaner anxiously awaits the moment of escape.

Conclusion: Long Distance horrormoaner tries to escape in a very unclever manner. PERMISSION DENIED!

Comments

*"Trash reading," refers to a teenage magazine of some sort.

So I made her eat lunch with Mr. Creature, Ms. Doppler, and me upstairs. By lunchtime, the novelty had begun to wear off a bit, and the others ate downstairs. She was antsy though, and tried to make an excuse to go find the other kids. We saw right through it. She wanted to return to the world that she was familiar with. Looking back, I think she was probably just as perplexed about my world as I was about hers.

Section X
Battle Through the Break

Setting: Innocent Bystandard wished to solemnly* enjoy the short period of time before the next class takes place. Horrormoaner is snagged and caged so this undefdifying** feat can be made at least hopeful.

Climax: Horrormoaner wants to escape and uses the old, "Can I go to the bathroom?" excuse. There is little validity*** to that statement, but either way, Innocent Bystandard is left alone.

Conclusion: Innocent Bystandard is disgusted by the utter amount of wasted time during one four hour period, and wants a refund.

Comments

*solemnly = sacredly

**undefdifying = unbelievable [I think this came from death-defying.]

***validity = truth

I was just waiting for the day to be over at this point. I hated wasting time, and to me that is exactly what was happening.

Section XI
Math Stemulants

Setting: Innocent Bystandard stays in math class seeking sanctuary from the utter disturbance of the century. Horrormoaner doesn't know quite what to think as the surroundings change and adjustment time was none.

Climax: Horrormoaner falls asleep (though Innocent Bystandard does not notice).

Conclusion: Sanctuary is lost when Innocent Bystandard is finished with exam.

Comments

Thank God it was a math day. Every other day, I got to go over to the high school for algebra class. I was the only one in the eighth grade, so my schedule was necessarily different from the other kids. Math was a double period, so it went from after lunch until the last period of the day. I felt a sense of satisfaction at her dissatisfaction, as though she were paying a debt for the behavior of herself and the other kids whose behavior I did not understand. She was in my world for a bit, and that felt good . . . But that changed when we had to go back.

| Math | + | Innocent Bystandard | = **Satisfaction**

| Math | + | Horrormoaner | = **Sleep**

| Sleep | + | Horrormoaner | = **Relief**

Section XII
Homeroom Horrormoaning

Setting: Long Distance horrormoaner unfortunately followed Innocent Bystandard back to uncivilized territory.

Climax: Long Distance moaner withdraws, for there are none of the former cronies present within the 50 foot vicinity. Innocent Bystandard is continually receiving many more earfuls from the omnipotent overseers*.

Conclusion: It's time for the Innocent Bystandard to leave (Long Distance horrormoaner is forced to go).

Comments

*Mr. Creature and Ms. Doppler

I think I was hoping I would lose her somewhere along the way back. I was in Ms. Doppler's homeroom, and there was not anybody in there with whom she had been causing trouble earlier. Unfortunately, the teachers still had what I perceived to be some grudge against me. They kept talking about it. I felt awful, and I was so glad the day was almost over.

Section XIII
Promotional PMS

Setting: All beings are preparing for promotion. The Innocent Bystandards are bored with the redundancy, while the horrormoaners still don't know what their role is (their focus is on a certain Long Distance horrormoaner).

Climax: None

Conclusion: All horrormoaners goof off during the class promotional exercises and get hollered at, while Innocent Bystandard pukes up redundant actions.

Comments

We spent days going through promotion exercises in preparation for the ceremony when we would officially graduate from middle school and become high school students. The kids had trouble anyway, but they had even more trouble with the additional distraction of my "friend."

Section XIV
Tearable Report

Setting: Horrormoaners just realized that the Long Distance moaner wasn't (isn't) from around here, and lives far off. Innocent Bystandard knows nothing.

Climax: Exchanges of everything from numbers* to toenail polish was made by the horrormoaners and the Long Distance moaner. Innocent Bystandard knows nothing.

Conclusion: Innocent Bystandard knows nothing.

Comments

*phone numbers

I was just ready to be done with the day. Apparently the kids did not realize that she still lived far away (and was going back). I remember she was supposed to come with me to babysit at the end of the day, but she decided not to come. I think her mother came and picked her up at the school, and that was then end of that. Thank God.

Section XV
Oh Boy!

Setting: Horrormoaners are all drooling. They never give up. They can't. Innocent Bystandards aren't well and have had enough horrormoaning.

Climax: She said that he likes her but he doesn't really, because she used him (as a foot rest) the last time. This time she's serious and he's sleepy but either way they're both gone with the breeze*. Innocent Bystandard falls face down with uncontrollable laughter.

Conclusion: Used again. Find another space.**

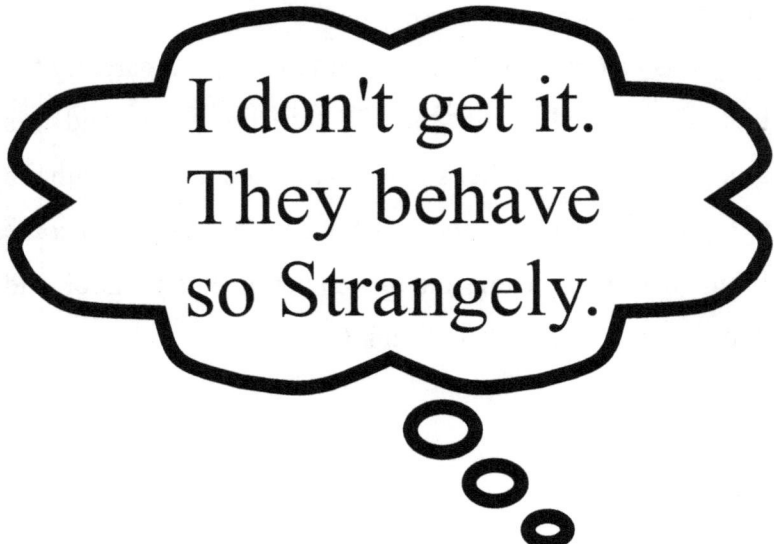

Comments

*"Gone with the breeze," is a reference to, *Gone with the Wind*.

**"Used again. Find another space," means: In the story above, the girlfriend was just using the boyfriend, so the conclusion was that he had to find some other place to go.

This is just more of the nonsense jabber I heard going on around me. Someone cheated on someone else, and no one ever seemed to learn, and all they seemed to do was talk about it. It was irritating.

Section XVI
Clothes Call!

Setting: Long Distance moaner sets the new trend for all other horrormoaners and horrormoaning SeeMeHearMes. They seem to enjoy the big, baggy, comfortable look better than the draws* down look. The Innocent Bystandard ignores the unworthy-of-their-attention situation.

Climax: A style trend switch was made tomorrow yesterday** and all horrormoaners now can go swimming in the lovesick clothing*** while Innocent Bystandard tries to convince themselves it's just a stage and they'll grow out of it.

Conclusion: Innocent Bystandard is getting grey hairs.

Comments

*draws = drawers [pronounced in a Maine accent], meaning pants

**"Made tomorrow yesterday," was just my playing around with words, trying to create a paradox to make the reading a bit more interesting.

***"Lovesick clothing," refers to the kind of clothing horrormoaners wore because they were so obsessed about their emotions. Somehow I saw the clothes as playing their own part in the drama.

This whole clothing thing was a stage I never went through. There were many stages that I never went through, or that I went through differently than other people. This is one of them.

NOTES

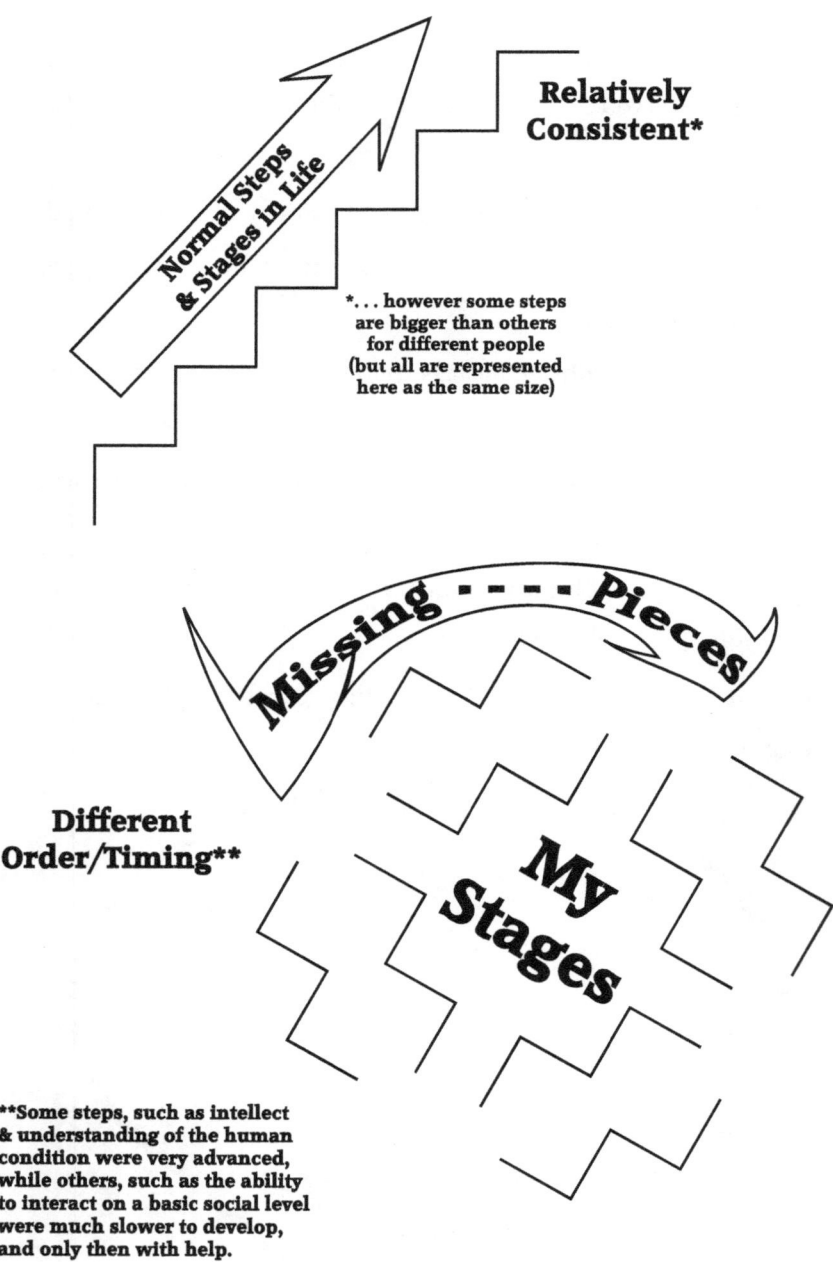

Section XVII
New News

Setting: Horrormoaner is yakking constantly at Innocent Bystandard about all their horrormoanal discoveries. Innocent Bystandard just sort of nods, with no more excitement than the bark off a dead tree.

Climax: Horrormoaner realized that he liked her so she told him that he said to her that she needed to go and do that for him because, well she didn't exactly know why, but that didn't matter. Innocent Bystandard trances.

Conclusion: Horrormoaner is so engulfed in her gossip that Innocent Bystandard gets off [the bus] and she ends up talking with the seat and going home with the bus driver.

Comments

The kids were trying to interact with me, especially after I had just brought one of their own kind to school. However, I did not recognize that at the time, nor did I know how to or really have much desire to interact with them.

The "trancing" refers the disconnection that occurred socially, especially when things got overwhelming. I did not understand social behavior very well to begin with, let alone complex teenage social behavior. When things got overwhelming I would often just check out and go off somewhere in my own mind. A high school teacher told me once, "Jessica, it's not fair that you're off visiting the Grand Canyon while everyone else is sitting here in class." Maybe not, but it is what I had to do to survive.

NOTES

Section XVIII

Avoiding Avengers

Setting: Innocent Bystandard tries unbelievably hard to avoid horrormoaner through telecommunications. Horrormoaner is persistent.

Climax: Horrormoaner finally unfortunately gets a hold of Innocent Bystandard.

Conclusion: Innocent Bystandard should never answer the phone.

Comments

After the trauma I had experienced at school, I did not want to talk to my friend anymore on the phone. I wanted to avoid the whole situation.

Section XIX
Phone Fright II

Setting: Horrormoaner calls Innocent Bystandard on the telephone. Innocent Bystandard is not the least (greatest or anything in between) bit excited.

Climax: Horrormoaner tells Innocent Bystandard they are not planning on heading back to their last residence.

Conclusion: Innocent Bystandard shakes head and superfluously gives up avoidance*.

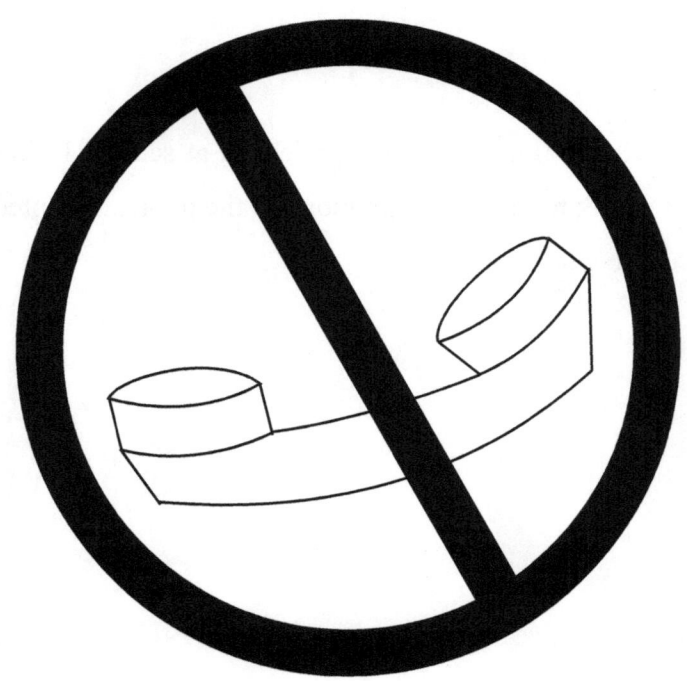

Comments

*"Superfluously gives up avoidance," means that left with no other options, the Innocent Bystandard (I.e., me) gives up trying to avoid her.

I did not want to talk to my friend anymore after what had occurred. I did not understand her, and there was a complete emotional disconnect. I wanted desperately to avoid her.

I remember that night I went to babysit, and I fell asleep after the kids went to bed. I was so overstimulated that my body had completely shut down. It took the parents of the kids over twenty minutes to wake me up when they got home.

NOTES

Horrormoaning In the Real World

Horrormoaning In the Real World

All of these stories are set in places around the community. They are imaginary with no concrete basis in actual events, unlike the previous two sets. However, they contain basically the same themes, including a great deal of social behavior that I did not understand and had no personal reference point for, and which my way of dealing with was mostly through avoidance. They are of interest since they build off the previous stories. Also, the language play can be further appreciated here.

This section illustrates that my confusion did not end at the end of the school day. It was always with me, and it still is to a greater or lesser extent, depending on the circumstances.

Section I	Clothes the Department Store
Section II	Theatre Throttling
Section III	Zip 'em Up at the Zoo
Section IV	Bakery Scare
Section V	Rash Feelings at the Doctor's Office
Section VI	Auditory Optometrists
Section VII	Derogatory Dentistry

Section VIII	Paralyzed at the Podiatrists
Section IX	Done Deal
Section X	School System Sagas
Section XI	House Visit
Section XII	As the General Story Goes
Section XIII	Pool your Bets
Section XIV	Bus your Stationary Thoughts Another Way
Section XV	The After Office
Section XVI	Shoe Them Away
Section XVII	Booksdoor
Section XVIII	Too Many Dogs in the Bark
Section XIX	Boring Cage of Thunder
Section XX	Men tally the Results!

Section I
Clothes the Department Store

Setting: Innocent Bystandard is casually browsing at everything taken to be important in life that the store carried. Horrormoaners were in the lingerie department doing who knows what.

Climax: Innocent Bystandard grows embarrassed by the utter thought of these disgusting actions taking place in the open. As if school wasn't bad enough. The activities being practiced were more graphic than these at school.

Conclusion: Pitiful. Simply pitiful.

Comments

I did not really like shopping, especially for clothes. Finding something that fit comfortably and that was appropriate to wear to school was always a challenge. I often got overstimulated looking. The exception to this was grocery stores, and toy stores when I was younger. I especially found underwear embarrassing. I did sometimes observe people in the underwear department, and even more, getting excited about it. I just did not understand, and I still do not understand.

Section II
Theatre Throttling

Setting: Innocent Bystandard, so not to be engrossed in the endless boredom of media madness, sells popcorn for the nearest theatre around with guaranteed money for a college education set aside. Horrormoaners walk in, in hopes to see the new soap opera movie. They redundantly rave about the results of its standings.

Climax: Innocent Bystandard, seeing the idiocracy* of the group, plots to get them kicked out of the theatre so that the show's ratings drop dramatically, and it heads out of the theatre—not even to make video cassettes.

Conclusion: Horrormoaners are simultaneously kicked out of every theatre in the country while Innocent Bystandards all over the nation plug this in as a wonderful experience.

Comments

*idiocracy = idiocy

I have never been very interested in movies. I get bored with them. I also do not like the unpredictable nature of them. I am more likely to want to go see a movie I have seen before, especially if I am with someone else, rather than one I have never seen before. Eighth grade was no exception.

My interests were definitely in going to college and making enough money for college. The other kids had very different interests than I did, (one of them being movies) and they all seemed pretty pointless. I just wanted to be the one who had control of what was going on. I wanted the power, and I wanted to show them how dumb their interests were.

Section III

Zip 'em Up at the Zoo

Setting: Innocent Bystandard is dragged to the zoo by a couple of clueless turnips to make them happy—though Innocent Bystandard still isn't sure why they're* putting themselves through this numbness. Horrormoaners are finding restless activities through the course of their imaginary journeys off to who knows where.

Climax: Horrormoaners are gawking at just about every zoo animal they can see. They just plain don't stop. Innocent Bystandard is growing sick throughout the situation.

Conclusion: Innocent Bystandard walks by each motormouth horrormoaner and zips up each of their jackets hoping they will take the hint**—realizing all the way that it is mission impossible.

Comments

*they're = Innocent Bystandard

** Zipping up their jackets was an analogy for zipping up their mouths. This is the hint I wanted them to take—to be quiet.

Sometimes I would go somewhere with someone if I was invited. Although I often regretted it if I ended up in a place that was either overstimulating or completely boring, which did happen from time to time, and happens even more now that I am older. In this story, the horrormoaner characters continue their usual crazy behaviors. And as usual, I just wished they would stop. I wanted them to be still and quiet.

Section IV
Bakery Scare

Setting: Bread's the word. Innocent Bystandard is, with a parent, shopping for fresh baked bread—though most of it has gone to mold. Horrormoaner (un)expectedly pops in.

Climax: Horrormoaner asked Innocent Bystandard rather openly if she said that he said because she'd heard that she did and didn't want the truth to be expressed*.

Conclusion: Innocent Bystandard, engrossed in their own thought, shrugs and says, guess so.

NOTES

Comments

*expressed = exposed

Going to the bread store was something special that I got to do with my parents when I was younger. I loved it. Not just getting to buy a lot of bread, but I loved the smell in the air. It relaxed me and filled up my senses. I could feel it throughout my whole body. It felt good.

In this story, some horrormoaner kid who I knew from school came in and started talking to me. I did not understand what she was talking about. I did not know what to say or how to interact.

I liked to be in my own world, and I got frustrated if I was interrupted. Agreeing was a great way to get people to go away. But often it was because I did not understand or I did not know what else to say, and other times it was because I could not process the information in the conversation because I had so much else going on inside my own mind, my own world. It was hard to know how to get someone to stop talking to me. People tended to get offended if I said, "Would you please stop talking and go away?"

Section V
Rash Feelings at the Doctor's Office

Setting: SeeMeHearMe is in to the doctor's office working on some sort of attention plea (nothing knew so far). Horrormoaner jaunts through the door, displaying detestable acts (still nothing knew)—at least they made it into a doctor's office where some (il)logical information may be presented to the horrormoaner. Innocent Bystandard nonchalantly steps in, taking long controlled strides, just observing and standing by (now at least there's something known).

Climax: SeeMeHearMe runs around with part of the body exposed showing of the skin irritation they somehow acquired. Horrormoaners clear up the attention deficit of the SeeMeHearMes by of course feeding them* until they're full—and more. Innocent Bystandard is pretending not to pay attention at all.

Conclusion: When the SeeMeHearMe irritation is gone (never...) horrormoaners once again flood the deficit**.

Comments

*"Feeding them" means giving them attention.
**the attention deficit

I saw that there were kids who loved to get attention by any means they could find. And then there were other kids, who loved giving those kids attention. And they loved touching each other, and since this idea pretty much repulsed me, I really could not understand why other people liked it. The whole big thing though was one major attention feast, and it never seemed to end. I always just stood by and watched. Even though I did not understand much of it at all, I always thought I was the one who knew what was going on.

I always saw myself as perfectly composed and in control (even when I was falling apart emotionally), an all-knowing observer on the side, thus the supposed nonchalant attitude and the long, controlled strides.

Section VI
Auditory Optometrists

Setting: The vision of the Innocent Bystandard is growing extremely blurry. Well-renowned SeeMeHearMe pops into the eye doctor's office because he thought he saw someone he knew (if he didn't it wouldn't matter anyway).

Climax: SeeMeHearMe follows Innocent Bystandard into the exam room just like a puppy dog.

Conclusion: Innocent Bystandard briefly explains to the doctor that this person's health is questionable, and when searching to find health help, he ended up in the wrong building for lack of following directions.

Comments

In this story, I was at the doctor's office when a kid from school saw me and came in to say hello. I did not want anything to do with him, but he was not taking my hints, and did not want to leave. I just figured he must have real mental problems since he could not understand that I did not want to be bothered.

And I always felt I had to make excuses for their behavior to adults, because they did not really seem to understand it either. I guess, the adults noticed that I was different and were able to connect to me intellectually because I did not have all the hormones and emotions getting in the way of my logical reasoning and processing, which are traits adults tend to connect with more readily than those of typical emotional teenagers.

Sometimes I felt responsible for giving the adults an explanation. Other times, I just shrugged my shoulders and sided with the adults because I was even more puzzled than they were. At least in the case of most adults, they were once teenagers who behaved like that. So somewhere inside them, they should be able to relate to the feelings of teenagers. Most adults just become disconnected and forget. I was just never connected in the first place.

Section VII
Derogatory Dentistry

Setting: Horrormoaner goes flying through the door of the dentist's office (3 hours late for their 9:00 appointment*), checks themselves in and by doctor's orders pays in advance. Innocent Bystandard also walks in, except their appointment is at 12:15. Innocent Bystandard rolls a long babbling speech off their tongue and refuses to pay in advance.

Climax: Moments after Innocent Bystandard checks in, he has started his appointment and is soon finished. Horrormoaner loudly (yet shyly) awaits their screw at the drill.

Conclusion: Innocent Bystandard is gone and horrormoaner is promptly kicked out of the dentist's office with flying colors at 5:00 when they took him to be a begging bum just off the street.

Comments

*It was 12:00.

I hated being told what to do. I still do. In this case, I did not want to prepay for services. So I talked my way out of it. I often did that when I was younger to avoid some penalty or to retain control of a situation in which I felt was out of my control.

And in this story, there was a horrormoaner kid who came late, and the dentist refused to treat him because his behavior was outrageous. This made me happy because I felt like through bringing this kid to justice, the horrormoaners were finally getting what they deserved in some way. I somehow saw this as payback for all their "strange" behavior.

NOTES

Section VIII
Paralyzed at the Podiatrists

Setting: Innocent Bystandard meets up with another Innocent Bystandard while waiting to have a wart removed. They are both itching for excitement and plan for a revolt and disposition* in the operating room.

Climax: Innocent Bystandards knock off their last doubts and are both in the same room to be operated on (imagine that!). To be redundant, they both have warts on the same foot (right side) and doctors are just now planning the procedure.

Conclusion: Doctors run out of the room frightened by the twisted use of vocabulary comprised** with the eye contact made throughout the sense of the matter***.

Comments

*disposition = demonstration

**comprised = combined

***"Throughout the sense of the matter," means, while discussing the procedure.

In this story I had an ally, a friend who understood me. There were still a few of my good "intellectual" friends left in eighth grade. I felt strongly connected to them, and they were great. However, they were also connected to and still doing things with the other kids who were behaving strangely. This I did not understand. And so even though I felt happy to be dominating the world with them, I still felt disconnected because although they were intellectual, they were also emotional. And this seemed to be a complete contradiction.

I.B.K.B.

Innocent Bystandard

Knows

Best

Section IX
Done Deal

Setting: SeeMeHearMe feels* it necessary to buy a new car as they come bolting through the entrance to the Generic Vehicle Association. Horrormoaner happens to be the clerk and is expressing their life(less) story to all.

Climax: All that the SeeMeHearMe wants is service—and Now. SeeMeHearMe goes buzzing around trying their best to make themselves known. Horrormoaners are still engulfed in their very own world of restless activities.

Conclusion: SeeMeHearMe ends up tearing the lot to pieces while searching for service as horrormoaner is emotionally disturbed by the atrocious break up of the two parties.

Comments

*The word choice of "SeeMeHearMe feels," is very interesting. Indeed, they were feeling, and functioning based on those feelings and emotions, in ways that I was unable to relate to and could not understand. I needed something or someone to help bridge the gap, at least to help me understand this was normal.

In this story, one kid was bouncing off the walls, and the other was just droning on about his miserable existence. They were both vying for the other's attention, and were relatively content to just continue talking. Somehow, even though they were engrossed in their own business, they could relate to and understand each other.

Section X
School System Sagas

Setting: Innocent Bystandard heads into office of school building to retrieve fan mail. Horrormoaners are, as usual, in yakking mode. Innocent Bystandard keeps to their self as they casually stretch by.

Climax: Horrormoaner (being older now) has learned to somewhat ignore the fantastic feats of the Innocent Bystandard. Innocent Bystandard decided to have a word with Omnipotent Overseer about the curriculum requirements for the coming school year. Horrormoaner, however, is utterly engrossed in her husband doing this when she specifically told him to do that.

Conclusion: Omnipotent Overseer is lured into the trap of the land of Testosterhome and Innocent Bystandard is forced to take control as they watch the other parties being dragged down to [the level of] that of the horrormoaner.

Comments

Mr. Creature and Ms. Doppler often had me go get their mail in the office, which they referred to as, "fan mail." They were pretty popular after all. After I got the mail and went back to the room, I found the desk of Mr. Creature, the Omnipotent Overseer, swarmed with students. They were likely dragging him into some drama, which I considered to be the land of Testosterhome. I somehow saw myself as the hero, rescuing the teacher from irritation and confusion.

NOTES

Section XI

House Visit

Setting: Plumber Call!

Climax: We don't want any!

Conclusion: Relief. . .

Comments

This was a horrormoaner dressed up as a plumber showing up at my house. I did not call for the plumber, and immediately saw that it was a horrormoaner trying to trick me. So I sent him away. What a relief.

Section XII
As the General Story Goes

Setting: Horrormoaners are finishing up their shift at the old Out Back store in Rough Neck Woods as Innocent Bystandard is simply passing through hunting for the next oasis. Supplies were needed as things were running low.

Climax: Innocent Bystandard cautiously walks into the store and finds the items needed as horrormoaners are heard doing the he said, she said thing. Innocent Bystandard didn't realize they were back so soon from their trip to Testosterhome (while they were gone, all was quiet on the Eastern Back*), otherwise the store would have stayed vacant as it was moments before Innocent Bystandard innocently entered. Innocent Bystandard quite innocently drops off items that weren't really needed after all and innocently walks out.

Conclusion: Horrormoaners determine Innocent Bystandard guilty thereby creating a paradox upon which is irrelevant because Innocent Bystandard said so.

Comments

*"All was quiet on the Eastern Back," refers to, *All Quiet on the Western Front*, one of my favorite novels at the time.

In this story, I walked into a store that seemed pretty quiet and low key. While I was in there shopping, rambunctious kids came in, and that was enough to overstimulate me and make me want to leave the store. There is absolutely nothing I need in a store when I become overstimulated. In this case, the kids seemed to take offense, since perhaps they were trying to interact with me and I just walked off. That was not unusual either. But, I was okay with it, and so that made it all okay.

Section XIII
Pool Your Bets

Setting: What a day for a swim. Ugh! The place is crawling with SeeMeHearMes. The horrormoaners have already done their arbitrary yodeling and escaped the premises.

Climax: Innocent Bystandard is incidentally, much relieved upon seeing a clean swimming environment. It's too bad though, that the pool was filthy and the sidewalks weren't fit to walk on. SeeMeHearMe is beyond repair.

Conclusion: As nightfall came, the pool began to clear, but it was suddenly filled with disgust.

Comments

In this story, I wanted to go swimming, but the pool was filled with kids who drove me nuts. So I waited. Then, by night time, I decided I did not actually want to go swimming anyway, probably because of the exhaustion of the anticipation and waiting all day long. In addition, knowing that noisy kids had been in there all day, I could still feel all the energy in the air, which is why the pool was filled with disgust. This was when I realized that the environment still was not going to work well as a place for me to swim.

This kind of anticipation was common in my everyday life. I would often think about an activity (such as a basketball game for example) for days. I would be devastated if it got canceled because I had spent so much time planning it and waiting for it. However, sometimes even if whatever I was waiting for did not get canceled, I would at times be too exhausted or overstimulated to participate because of all the anticipation (and often anxiety), leading up to it.

Section XIV
Bus Your Stationary Thoughts Another Way

Setting: Innocent Bystandards have lowered themselves to other means of transportation by which the town folks move. Knowing more than well what they are getting into, they proceed with the plan. Aloner* horrormoaners and SeeMe-HearMes await their presence.

Climax: The schedule of travels was the most senseless thing ever read by the Innocent Bystandards. A SeeMe-HearMe horrormoaner approached the confused Bystandards and reads the schedule simply giving explanation as to why it was as it was.

Conclusion: It's interesting to know they're good for something.

Comments

*"Aloner" means the Horrormoaners and SeeMeHearMes who were by themselves, without their friends.

In this story, I was on the city bus with a group of friends who I could still tolerate. The bus schedule did not make any sense, and it was difficult to read. However, the kids who rode the city bus all the time knew why the schedule was the way it was and were able to explain it to us, which I found very helpful.

This was one way I could connect with the other kids, if they came into my world and engaged me in something I was interested in. However, this was difficult to do because my interests were so very limited and albeit very different than most of my peers. The topic of schedules is one thing that still gets my attention though.

Section XV

The After Office

Setting: Horrormoaner is trying to figure out the meaning of mailing a letter. Innocent Bystandard doesn't even wish to touch the tissue at nose*.

Climax: Innocent Bystandard happens to land themselves behind the horrormoaner. The letter handed to the lettertaker** is certainly one interpretation. However, most likely not the U.S. Government's interpretation.

Conclusion: Innocent Bystandard exits in awe.

Comments

*tissue at nose = issue at hand

**lettertaker = postal clerk

In this story, I was behind a stupid kid at the post office. He wanted to mail a letter, but the material he had was either incomplete or inappropriate, and it was not able to be sent through the mail. I just left dumbfounded, unable to even do what I had gone there for.

I found a majority of behaviors distracting and intolerable, rudeness and incompetence to name a couple. When I would run across people who exhibited these behaviors, I would obsess about the behavior and then become overstimulated. At this point, I would have to take a break from the situation and come back to it at a later point in time.

Section XVI
Shoe Them Away

Setting: Footwear . . . how exciting. Innocent Bystandard hates to hunt for sneakers. The catch is usually few and far between. Horrormoaners on the other hand are pumped up and ready to spike a hot deal.

Climax: Horrormoaners have a son. One of which they pay no attention to, causing the child to behave as a SeeMe-HearMe. Horrormoaners realize their child has no shoes. They figure they need to swing by there* anyways because one of the pairs of shoes they had for Monday** wasn't suiting them. Innocent Bystandard can see it coming and concludes that . . .

Conclusion: . . . shoes can wait until another gloomy day.

Comments

*"There," refers to the shoe store.

**Having a pair of shoes for Monday implies having a different pair of shoes for every day of the week.

    I hated shoe shopping. I still do. It was always hard to find something that would fit my feet just right, and something that I would wear. Also, shoe stores had too many choices, and most of them were wrong. So I felt like I was searching through a bunch of wrong choices looking for a correct answer. It was overwhelming. I just left the store feeling frustrated and overstimulated, as often happened when what I needed was not right there and the environment was too stimulating for me to handle. I made observations here about people who came into the shoe store and actually bought shoes, and even enjoyed being in the shoe store. That was something I really could not relate to.

Section XVII
Booksdoor

Setting: Horrormoaner is into the bookstore (irreguardless* of the fact they should be ban** in public places and use of "normal"*** facilities). Anyway, Innocent Bystandard needs to find out if their piece of work is out on the shelves earlier than projected—as it should be.

Climax: Horrormoaner comes over and tries to get a rise out of Innocent Bystandard. Innocent Bystandard smiles with delight.

Conclusion: Horrormoaner . . . your the next contaminant on the Rise is tight****.

Comments

*I insisted on using the word, "irreguardless," mostly in fact, because it is not a word.

**ban = banned

***Normal: Anything Innocent Bystandard (me) considers to be so.

****The "next contaminant on the Rise is tight," refers to, the "next contestant on the *Price is Right*."

    I was a perfectionist, and I had a lot of goals, writing and publishing books being one of them. I did not think noisy kids should go to bookstores, especially the bookstores I liked to go to. I was able to get a bit of revenge at the end of the story though, which brought some satisfaction.

Section XVIII

Too Many Dogs in the Bark

Setting: Innocent Bystandard wishes to go and enjoy a nice afternoon in the park. Hah! Right . . . SeeMeHearMe horrormoaners are also present. They are engaging in disgusting activities. All of which aren't worth heading off on a tangent on*.

Climax: NONE

Conclusion: Park becomes over flooded with plenty of fish in the sea** and Innocent Bystandard decides to go home.

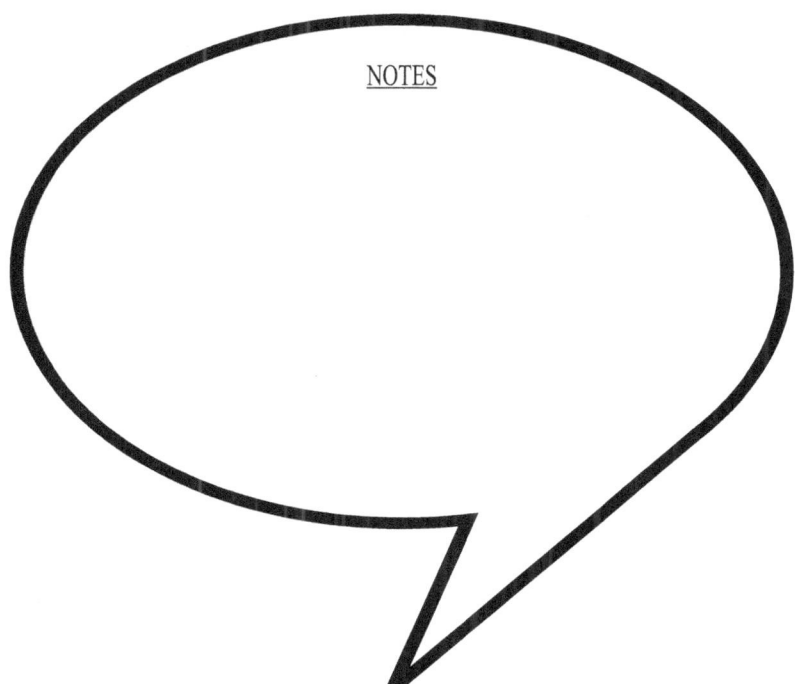

NOTES

Comments

*None of which are worth going off on a tangent about

**"Plenty of fish in the sea," is a reference to when someone is brokenhearted, and someone tells them, "Don't worry, there are plenty of fish in the sea." I saw the horrormoaners as the fish.

Again, I wanted to go somewhere (the park), but because of the overstimulating environment that was created by the noisy and obnoxious people who were there, I had to decide to either leave or ignore whatever was going on and try it. I decided to try it, but when that did not work, because all the horrormoaning people were there all over each other, it became too much for me, and I had to go home.

This was definitely a common occurrence. There were many things I wanted to do, but could not do when there were too many people or when there was too much going on in the environment.

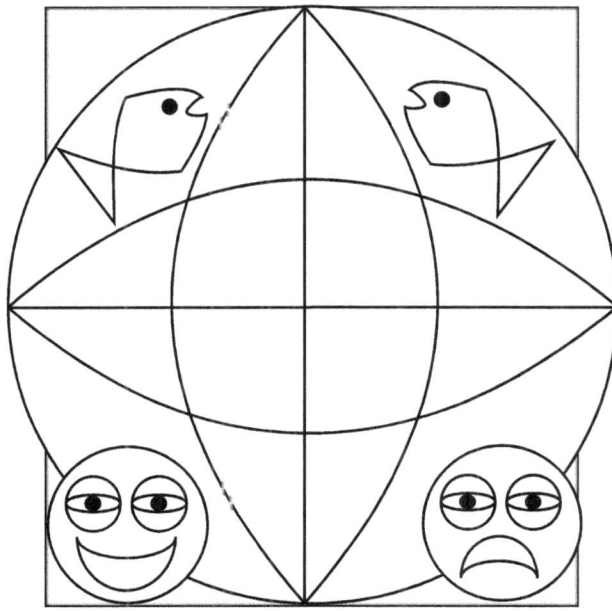

The World

it means

The Sea

[Fish = People]

Plenty of Fish in the Sea
=
Many People in the World

Section XIX
Boring Cage of Thunder

Setting: The Innocent Bystandard decides to take a trip to the amusement park. They arrive with another Innocent Bystandard, and things actually look okay. The atmosphere for once feels normal.

Climax: Innocent Bystandards decide to go about their business, expecting to see horrormoaners, SeeMeHearMes, or anybody. Nothing peaks.

Conclusion: Innocent Bystandard sighs peacefully as the geometry teacher rambles on about trapezoids.

Comments

This was too good to be true. And it was. This was only in my imagination. When I came back to reality, I was in geometry class hearing about trapezoids. I would have loved to have been able to go somewhere fun with a friend, and not be overstimulated. That very rarely happened, and less and less the older I got.

Section XX
Men tally the Results!

Setting: An auction. How stupid, the Innocent Bystandard thought with a polite gaze in their eyes**. Like I want to buy some idiot's train set or bicycle or something. And, oh great. To top it all off, the SeeMeHearMes are up front pointing and ranting and raving and everything else.

Climax: Horrormoaners show up and just can't beat the SeeMeHearMes to the win of an item.

Conclusion: Finally a horrormoaner pays $500 for a can of hairspray. The SeeMeHearMe, seeing their unvictory*, for once smiles smugly. It's all in their head.

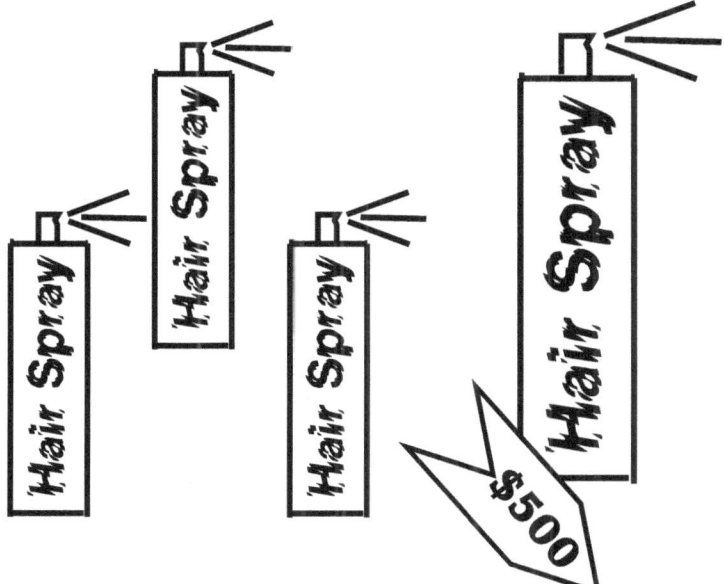

Comments

In this story, I am at an auction. There is no way I can compete with the kids who naturally make noise every day to get what they want. And in this case, the very emotional kids are so attached to needing hair spray that they will pay such a high price for it. Most of them were not that good at math anyway.

*The attention seekers were pleased that the other kids stupidly spent so much money on such a silly purchase, and considered this to be a victory. It was not really that important though, and not much of a victory, thus an "unvictory," that was all in their heads.

**"How stupid, the Innocent Bystandard thought with a polite gaze in their eyes." This is a great way to express what I felt a lot of times.

*And a fitting end to this set of stories
as I stare out at the world . . .*

The End

NOTES

About the Author

Jessica was born in Maine, USA. She is currently a teacher and writer, working in Japan. She loves spending time with her family and practicing karate and judo. Although never formally diagnosed with Asperger syndrome, she has experienced problems with socialization and communication, and so she is easily able to relate to others who experience these things. She has overcome many of her difficulties and has learned the language to better communicate what she is thinking and feeling. She has been of great help to many families by giving them suggestions as well as priceless insight into their children. Please feel free to contact her.

Check out her web page, and personal blog for more information and updates on this and other projects.

Jessica R. Dunton

Telephone: (617) 297-2543
E-mail: Sensoryintegrate@sensoryintegrate.com
Web Page: www.sensoryintegrate.com
Blog: www.aspergerandme.blogspot.com

www.ingramcontent.com/pod-product-compliance
Lightning Source LLC
LaVergne TN
LVHW011350080426
835511LV00005B/223